The POWER of THERAPY

The POWER of THERAPY

How to Navigate Change, Transform Trauma, and Make Sense of Your Mental Health Care

Joshua Newman, LPCC

ISBN (print, soft cover): 978-1-7369239-0-0
ISBN (ebook): 978-1-7369239-1-7
ISBN (audiobook): 978-1-7369239-2-4

Published by Mountain Stream Books, Albuquerque, New Mexico

For my clients—

You are my ultimate inspiration.

Contents

Author's Note 1

Introduction 3

PART I: Getting Oriented 9

1. Why See a Shrink? 11
2. How to Find *Your* Therapist 15
3. What to Expect from Therapy 25
4. Client Participation Is Required 33
5. How Therapy Affects Others in Your Life 41
6. Therapy Timelines 43
7. What's Not Supposed to Happen in Therapy 47

PART II: The Journey 53

8. Maps and Guidance: Finding Direction in Unfamiliar Terrain 55
9. Travel Gear: Get Outfitted for the Journey Ahead 61
10. Beyond Personality—Exploring the Psyche 69

11. Ego, Self-Deception, and the Courage to Change 77
12. Happiness Reconsidered 83
13. The Big Picture: Values, Purpose, and Meaning 89
14. The Hero's Journey 97
15. Insight and Action: How to Reach Your Full Potential 101
16. Nature: The Healing Power of the Great Outdoors 105
17. Dreams: The Forgotten Ally 111

PART III: Relationships 119

18. Yourself: Finding Peace Within 121
19. Family: "Tell me about your mother." 127
20. Lovers: The Eternal Quest for Companionship 133
21. How to Date Smarter and Date Faster 143
22. Conflict: It's Not as Bad as You Think 149
23. Estrangement: The End of the Road 155

PART IV: Issues Commonly Addressed in Therapy 159

24. Addictions 161
25. Attention-Deficit/Hyperactivity Disorder 165
26. Anger 169
27. Anxiety 173
28. Autism and Asperger Syndrome 177
29. Bipolar Disorder 181
30. Codependency 185
31. Depression 189
32. Difficult People 193
33. Grief and Loss 195
34. Guilt and Shame 197

35. Life Transitions 201
36. Obsessive-Compulsive Disorder 203
37. Parenting Concerns 207
38. Personality Disorders 211
39. Procrastination 215
40. Relationship Problems 219
41. Self-Destructive Behavior 223
42. Self-Esteem Problems 225
43. Trauma and PTSD 229

A Hopeful Future 237
End Notes 239
Further Reading 245
Acknowledgments 249
About the Author 253

Author's Note

THROUGHOUT THE BOOK, the terms *therapy*, *psychotherapy*, and *counseling* are used interchangeably. Each term refers to the practice of talk therapy, whereby a therapist and a client work together toward the resolution of psychological problems, the pursuit of personal goals, and the creation of improved mental health.

The profession of psychotherapy has never settled upon a solid preference for the term *client* or *patient* in reference to the person receiving services. Perhaps this ambivalence regarding terminology reflects the unique space that mental health care occupies.

In cases involving debilitating panic attacks, suicidal depression, bipolar disorder, schizophrenia, life-threatening addictions, and so forth, the therapist is providing crucial, often lifesaving health care services for their *patients*. In cases involving relationship turmoil, emotional malaise, existential dread, confusion over career direction, and many of the other reasons that bring people into therapy, the term *client* has a more familiar ring.

At the end of the day, the terms *client* and *patient* are used interchangeably. I have chosen to use the term *client*, as it is how I most often refer to the people I serve.

Throughout the book, I tell stories of clients, drawn from the lives of real people, that are used to illustrate various concepts. In order to completely protect the confidentiality of my clients, I have created composites of various individuals I have known—both personally and professionally—over the years. No example represents any one individual. Accordingly, the names used have all been created specifically for this book.

Introduction

YOU MAY HAVE picked up this book for many reasons. Perhaps you want to know if therapy really works. Maybe you have loved ones who have worked with a counselor, and you feel a mix of curiosity and skepticism about the practice. Or perhaps someone in your life has encouraged—or even insisted—that you get help, but you aren't sure how to begin.

Or maybe you have been burned by a bad therapy experience in the past. Your parents dragged you to see a counselor when you were a kid and you hated it, or you and your spouse saw a therapist and things quickly went south. Whatever happened, it made you feel discouraged and left you wondering if therapy had anything to offer you.

Or maybe you are a therapy veteran and always on the lookout for books and resources to help you to go deeper and farther into your therapeutic experience.

The good news is, if you see yourself in any of these descriptions, you're in the right place. In this book, you will gain access to vital insider information on every aspect of the therapy experience—everything from the ins and outs of contacting a therapist for the first time, to insights about how therapy can help you address issues such as anxiety, depression, addiction, and trauma.

As your guide, I will walk you through the core principles of change, offer you a window into contemporary perspectives on healthy relationships, and provide you with ample resources for many of the specific issues that require mental health care. No matter where you are on your therapy journey, this book will help you figure out your next step.

If you're new to therapy, you may wonder what actually happens inside a therapist's office. Many clients describe their experience of therapy as life changing. Tears of catharsis flow, releasing previously blocked energy. Emotional release gives way to feelings of peace. Despair transforms into laughter. Goals are identified and, with hard work, they are met. Over the course of many hours, in a cozy therapy office (or over a Zoom screen), you and your therapist form a bond like no other. You become allies on the journey of healing and change.

Whether you are looking for help for something simple, such as stress management, or you are dealing with the emotional complexities of grief and loss, therapy has something to offer nearly everyone. Through the pages of this book, I give you an inside look at therapy—including how it works and why it works. Many of your questions will be answered, and you will find a wealth of insights and practical advice. This book can help you bring the power of therapy into your life.

MY PROFESSIONAL PATH

I consider myself tremendously lucky in my experiences as a professional therapist. Over the course of my career, I have had the opportunity to work with hundreds of kind, intelligent, and courageous people. I have had the privilege of working with individuals from all walks of life—artists, musicians, teachers, medical professionals, lawyers, professors, clergy, automotive professionals, tattoo artists, engineers, parents, retirees, teenagers, and college students. Many clients have come to me during times of crisis or transition; others have come because of an internal drive to learn more about themselves. I have learned a great deal about what really works through my relationships with my clients, and to them I am deeply grateful.

My clinical philosophy is what you might call East-West. While Western psychology has given us tremendous insights into the human mind, I have always been drawn to the wisdom of the East. As a result, you will find references to both meditation and Eastern thought sprinkled throughout the book. In my experience, it helps to cast a wide net while on your quest for greater mental health.

Psychotherapy, while guided by theory and research, is in essence an art form. I was very lucky to find a good mentor early in my career, who helped me to hone my craft. First with formal supervision sessions, and later with meandering conversations over sushi lunches, William Symes's influence upon my thought process and clinical strategy has been truly profound. Many of the concepts described in this book come directly out of our many hours of conversation and consultation.

PERSONAL EXPERIENCE WITH THERAPY

I also know what it's like to be a client. Throughout my adulthood, I have sought the help of mental health professionals at key inflection points in my life. I first sat down with a therapist at the age of twenty-four while I was in graduate school. In the years since, I have pursued counseling from a number of other clinicians; in some cases, the therapy was brief, while at other times, it was more in depth.

As a whole, my experiences with therapy nicely mirror the bell curve. A couple of my therapists were not helpful (one rambled on about himself for the entirety of the first session; another flooded me with reams of paperwork but had little substance to offer when we finally sat down to work). Two of my therapists were absolutely life changing. And the remainder were perfectly adequate, providing what I needed at the time.

Not only did my therapy experiences help me personally, they also showed me firsthand the trust, vulnerability, and grit required to get help. I know how it feels to be on both sides of the couch.

WHY I WROTE THIS BOOK

I am not only familiar with both sides of the couch. I am also passionate about the power of therapy to change lives. Time and again, I have watched in awe as my clients experience profound transformations. Therapy allows you to overcome challenges, face demons, heal trauma, deepen relationships, embark upon new careers, and ultimately become more fully yourself. As a result, I want to share my love of therapy with as many people as possible. This book's purpose is to remove obstacles from your path, while providing you with expert guidance along your way, thus increasing your odds of a favorable therapy outcome.

After two decades of clinical practice, I feel that I have a good lay of the land. I've attended conferences, participated in consultation groups, read countless books, and had lots of stimulating conversations with colleagues and mentors about how therapy really works. I have sorted through the wide variety of therapies offered today, attempting to isolate the signal from the noise. From this vantage point, I am in a position to help you get the most out of your experience of therapy. Think of me as your backcountry guide.

HOW TO USE THIS BOOK

Designed as a guidebook, this volume provides an A-to-Z overview of the entire process of psychotherapy. Feel free to read it cover to cover, or simply pick and choose the chapters that apply to your situation.

I divided the book into four parts. **Part I: Getting Oriented** is a comprehensive overview of the entire counseling process. Written for both therapy virgins and therapy veterans alike, it addresses many frequently answered questions and is chock full of practical suggestions. Included are tips for finding a therapist, making sense of the various mental health licenses, and optimizing your therapy experience.

You will also find guidance regarding what you might want to talk about in therapy, as well as information about the various forms of therapy that you might experience. I will help you troubleshoot common problems that can arise on your counseling journey, as well as address the question of how to know when it's time to change therapists. As you read, keep an eye out for **Pro Tips**—these are boxes with special advice about how to get the most out of therapy.

Part II: The Journey is a deep dive into the principles of change. Designed to be comprehensive while avoiding one-size-fits-all thinking, this section will shine a light on the many paths to psychological health and give you some ideas about what you'd like to explore and how you'd like to explore it. I begin with an overview of the assessment process, providing you with a roadmap for your journey. From there, our journey will take us down many trails, each one offering unique perspectives on your psychology.

As you delve into the chapters, you will encounter philosophical concepts, clinical observations, direct suggestions, examples of how others have made changes, and techniques to try out for yourself. Throughout the book, there are several **Ask Your Therapist** boxes, which are specifically designed to deepen your conversations with your therapist. Taken as a whole, these chapters are designed to help you better understand and accelerate your journey of change.

Part III: Relationships is devoted entirely to examining the relationships in your life. Beginning with an invitation to get better acquainted with yourself, you will be given tools and concepts for enriching your inner life, as well as guidance for tending to the wounds of childhood, sage advice from today's top relationship experts, and an introduction to conflict resolution skills.

You will also find chapters on dating strategy as well as the thorny issue of relationship estrangement. Whatever your relationship status, you are sure to find insights and information here that will help you enhance the most important relationships in your life.

Part IV: Issues Commonly Addressed in Therapy contains an overview of many of the issues that bring my clients into therapy, from ADHD to life transitions to trauma. Each chapter offers practical guidance and helpful information for whatever ails you, providing a historical context as well as current trends in evidence-based practices. Should you find that you want to go deeper into any given subject covered in this part, see **Further Reading** for suggested resources.

Whether you are contemplating going into therapy for the first time, or have seen more therapists than you can count, this book is sure to have something for you.

PART I

Getting Oriented

"Life is not what it's supposed to be. It's what it is.
The way you cope with it is what makes the difference."

–Virginia Satir, psychotherapist

Chapter One

Why See a Shrink?

Why bother to see a therapist? As many people will be quick to point out, you can talk to friends and family about your troubles, and they won't charge you a cent. You could also approach a trusted elder such as a teacher, coach, spiritual leader, or family friend. Or, better yet, tell your pet all about your problems. Dogs and cats are some of the best listeners—very patient, with a completely nonjudgmental attitude. Chances are, you could find any of these folks to be wise and caring listeners. There is no doubt that you can get emotional support and helpful advice from someone you already know and trust.

But while all of this is true, it's likely that you have run into the limitations of using existing relationships to help you through life's thorniest problems.

How often have you approached a loved one with a problem because you just wanted someone to listen, but instead, they jumped into problem-solving mode, giving you unwanted advice? Or perhaps, after pouring your heart out, they responded with a similar story from their life, taking the focus off of you and your concerns. Let's face it, we've all experienced these failures of empathy as we have tried to lay down our burdens upon friends and family, which is probably why you picked up this book.

There is something uniquely positive—and, in the best of cases, transformational—about what happens between therapist and client. And while there may be some mystery and magic to the therapy process, there are some clearly definable elements that work together to make therapy effective. The core elements of psychotherapy are objectivity, empathy, psychological insight, skills development, and the potential for a corrective emotional experience.

OBJECTIVITY

Unlike friends or family, a professional therapist is able to bring an objective point of view to your situation. This alone can be reason enough to talk to a professional. It can be incredibly helpful to vent about stress, process interpersonal conflicts, explore difficult family dynamics, and discuss other such concerns with someone who is removed from the issues at hand.

Having this kind of private, secure, and nonjudgmental interaction can allow you to speak and think more freely. Furthermore, an objective point of view can help you to arrive at important decisions more quickly and with greater clarity. Like a photographer with a wide array of lenses, a therapist can help you to view your situation from many different angles, providing focus, clarity, and perspective.

EMPATHY

An effective therapist is able to tune into your emotional state; they know how to express care and understanding in a way that connects directly with your experience. Combining objectivity with a warm, empathic attitude offers you both validation and support. Like a warm blanket on a cold winter's night, empathy provides comfort during the harsh storms life can dish out. Empathy alone is not sufficient to solve all problems, but it has consistently been shown to be a necessary ingredient for a successful therapy outcome.

PSYCHOLOGICAL INSIGHT

When you choose to work with a mental health professional, you gain access to someone who has dedicated their life to studying the human condition. A therapist's knowledge and experience allows them to provide you with insightful solutions that can accelerate change. Developing a relationship with someone who has a deep understanding of psychological principles—including personality structure, motivation, human behavior, and the nature of the unconscious mind—can be quite helpful during times of confusion and difficulty. In this way, a therapist is like an expert backcountry guide, helping you navigate challenging and unfamiliar terrain.

SKILLS DEVELOPMENT

Therapy frequently involves the development of new emotional skills. A therapist can share with you their toolbox of techniques for self-care and for coping with difficulties, resolving conflict, and developing healthy relationships. From cognitive behavioral exercises to mindfulness training, there are literally hundreds of practices and interventions that a therapist can offer for your benefit.

In addition to skills you can utilize to improve your mental health, a therapist also has a wealth of practical tips for developing healthy interpersonal relationships. I have spent many sessions in the role of relationship coach, helping my clients address relationship issues and practice difficult conversations. You can think of your therapist as a personal trainer for the mind, helping you to develop new strength while keeping you accountable to your goals.

CORRECTIVE EMOTIONAL EXPERIENCE

Finally—and perhaps most importantly—psychotherapy offers the potential for a corrective emotional experience. What, you may ask, is a corrective relationship experience? Quite simply, it is an experience of healing that occurs through the relationship between counselor and client.

We have all felt various degrees of pain and disappointment in our relationships with others. Such emotional injuries fall on a spectrum that ranges from minor conflicts and misunderstandings to profound abuse and neglect. A successful client-therapist relationship has the potential to provide profound emotional healing through the therapeutic relationship. While a corrective relationship experience cannot replace a troubled childhood, it can offer you the emotional validation vital to healing and moving forward.

MOVING FORWARD

As you can see, working with a well-trained therapist offers a host of unique and powerful benefits. That being said, the decision to get help requires a significant degree of trust. In order for therapy to be successful, you will need to be emotionally honest and vulnerable. Venturing into vulnerable spaces requires a combination of both courage and trust—and that means both trust in your therapist as well as trust in the journey itself.

It may give you comfort to know that professional therapists are licensed by a state board of examiners only after completing an advanced degree and receiving years of clinical supervision. Once fully licensed, therapists are required to complete many hours of continuing education each year. Furthermore, therapists are legally and ethically bound to do no harm. This includes maintaining strict confidentiality, among many other principles of ethical practice.

While licensure and training are important, in order for the alchemy of therapy to work, you must find someone who is a good match for you. Effective therapy depends upon a balanced working relationship between counselor and client. This is achieved through a combination of rapport and respect. In the next chapter, I explore how to find a therapist who is the right match for you.

Chapter Two

How to Find *Your* Therapist

Finding a therapist can feel overwhelming—especially if you are already emotionally distressed and have little bandwidth for doing research. Once you commit to the search, you might also run into discouraging situations, like reaching out to potential therapists, only to encounter unreturned phone calls and long waiting lists. But no matter your situation, there's no reason to despair. Once you have determined that you are ready to talk to someone, there can be no stopping you. With focus and persistence, you can find the right therapist to work with.

In order to expedite the goal of getting you onto a therapy couch—or perhaps a telehealth computer screen—we must first take the guesswork out of both locating and choosing a therapist. This chapter provides you with practical advice and insider information to help you get started with therapy as quickly as possible.

HOW TO FIND A THERAPIST

The three most reliable ways to locate a therapist are (1) word-of-mouth recommendation, (2) internet search, and (3) obtaining a list of in-network clinicians from your health insurance provider.

Nothing beats a word-of-mouth recommendation, which will give you an idea of a particular therapist's strengths, focus, and style. So the best way to start looking for a therapist is by simply asking around. Do you know anyone who is currently in therapy or who has done counseling in the past? If they had a good experience, get the name of their therapist. Don't hesitate to ask your friends, family, or your primary care provider.

You can also go online to find help; the internet has made locating a therapist easier than ever before. Many therapists have a professional website or a professional profile on a therapy website. I am personally a big fan of the *Psychology Today* user interface; you can filter your search by zip code, gender, insurance accepted, issues treated, populations served, and a whole host of other variables.

Viewing websites and online profiles can quickly give you a feel for someone. Pay attention to their training and their treatment philosophy, as well as the language they use to describe their clinical approach. These descriptions can provide some clues to both their personality and their clinical style.

Additionally, there are other, lesser-used routes for locating a therapist. Some employers offer an Employee Assistance Program (EAP), which provides free, short-term counseling (typically five to eight sessions). If there is a college or university in your town, you can also try calling the psychology department. Psychology faculty sometimes have a part-time private practice and are often well acquainted with therapists in the area.

Pro Tip: Reaching Out

When making contact with a potential therapist, it helps to be organized. In many cases, you will be leaving a voice mail. In addition to leaving your name and phone number, tell them what kind of insurance you have and a brief summary (a couple of sentences is enough) about why you are seeking therapy.

If they have a waiting list, and you want to work with them, ask to be added to it. You can keep searching for other therapists in the meantime.

Let the therapist know if your schedule happens to be flexible. Many counselors appreciate the opportunity to quickly fill a cancellation. If you can come in at the drop of the hat, it might just speed up how quickly you will get seen.

LICENSE TYPES: MAKING SENSE OF MENTAL HEALTH CREDENTIALS

What's the difference between a psychiatrist and a psychologist? Are counselors and therapists the same thing? Does it matter what kind of professional you see? Let's take a minute to answer these frequently asked questions.

During the time of Sigmund Freud, patients were seen by *psychiatrists* (medical doctors who specialize in mental illness) for lengthy psychoanalysis. In today's insurance-driven marketplace, the majority of psychiatrists focus primarily on providing assessments, acute care, and medication management. Very few psychiatrists still engage in traditional psychotherapy (also known as talk therapy).

During the twentieth century, *psychologists* (practitioners with a doctoral degree in psychology) made up the majority of practicing therapists. Today, master's level therapists (*counselors, social workers,* and *marriage and family therapists*) comprise the majority of therapists providing psychotherapy services.

Psychotherapy can be performed by a counselor, social worker, marriage and family therapist, psychologist, or psychiatrist. A *therapist* is a general term for a fully licensed mental health professional and commonly refers to psychologists, social workers, and counselors who provide psychotherapy.

According to a host of studies, the license type of your therapist does not influence therapy outcomes. There are, however, some circumstances in which it is advisable to seek out a specific kind of mental health professional. For example, if a serious mental illness is suspected (schizophrenia, bipolar disorder, severe depression), contacting a psychiatrist or psychiatric provider is recommended, as medication therapy will most likely be an essential component of your treatment plan.

If you are seeking couples or marriage counseling, you will want to contact either a licensed marriage and family therapist or a therapist with specialized training in counseling for couples.

And finally, if a thorough and comprehensive psychological assessment is required, a clinical psychologist or clinical neurologist who specializes in testing and assessments should be your first call.

However, for the vast majority of mental health concerns (anxiety, depression, stress management, life transitions, interpersonal challenges), the licensure type of the therapist has no bearing upon the effectiveness of therapy.

THE ABCS OF THERAPY: MAKING SENSE OF ALL THE ACRONYMS

In your search for a therapist, you may encounter terms such as *psychoanalysis*, *cognitive behavioral therapy* or *CBT*, *existential therapy*, *client-centered therapy*, *ACT*, *DBT*, *EMDR*, and many others. These are but a sampling of the dozens of theoretical orientations and branded techniques in existence today. As a matter of fact, there are a staggering number of acronyms for the different theoretical orientations being utilized in the modern era, with new ones emerging all of the time.

But wait! Before your head starts to swim, you don't need to worry about all of these terms. Most therapists are what are known as *integrated practitioners*, meaning they are trained in a variety of techniques. Effective therapists blend a combination of evidence-based theories and interventions, in a flexible manner, in order to best serve the needs of each individual client. Research has consistently found that the theoretical orientation of the clinician has little to no impact upon therapy outcomes. So unless you are looking for a specific kind of therapy, don't get bogged down by all of the acronyms.

THE PROS AND CONS OF SPECIALISTS VERSUS GENERALISTS

Many therapists have a general practice in which they address a broad range of concerns. These therapists are called *generalists*. Many other therapists, called *specialists*, prefer to focus only on specific problems and specific populations.

It can be argued that generalists have something unique to offer in terms of seeing a bigger picture. On the other hand, specialists benefit from having a deeper toolkit in their area of expertise. Examples of issues that, in many cases, are best addressed by seeing a specialist include ADHD, autism, addictions, bipolar disorder, eating disorders, and severe PTSD. Other areas of specialization include fertility issues, grief and loss, gender identity, men's issues, women's issues, and so forth.

I consider myself to be a generalist, with certain areas of special focus. My practice is approximately 90 percent adults and 10 percent adolescents. About 85 percent of my work is with individuals; the remaining 15 percent are couples and families. I see about an equal number of women and men. LGBTQ+ individuals make up a large percentage of my caseload, a development that happened organically over time.

I provide short-term, solution-oriented therapy for clients who want to focus on a single issue and who have no interest in delving into their past. I also do an extensive amount of long-term work with clients who are eager to know themselves at a deeper level, who seek to transform their lives in significant ways.

Like your family doctor, who addresses a broad range of medical concerns, I see a wide variety of people in my practice. Over the years, I have found that working with a range of issues allows me to stay nimble. For example, I frequently transfer insights from my individual work into my work with couples and vice versa.

If you are trying to decide which type of therapist to see, there are pros and cons of both specialists and generalists. ***When in doubt, ask your prospective therapist any questions you have about their level of experience in working with your particular issue.*** Every time you ask a question, you are creating a valuable opportunity to learn more about a potential therapist and, more importantly, to get a feel for how they relate to you.

TAKING A THERAPIST'S DEMOGRAPHIC PROFILE INTO ACCOUNT

In some cases, you may explicitly want to see a person with a specific demographic profile. This could include a therapist of a particular age, sex, race, sexual orientation, or any other number of personal variables that matter to you.

Perhaps you are looking to work with either a male or a female therapist. Common reasons for this include

- Preference for a therapist of the same sex to make it easier to discuss certain topics
- A therapist of the opposite sex to help you get a man's or woman's point of view on a situation
- Working on mother/father issues and wanting a therapist of the same sex as the parent you wish to address
- If you happen to relate better to men or women

In some cases, you may want a therapist of a particular age. Early in my career, when I was in my mid-20s, I worked at a community mental health center where my clients were assigned to me at random. At the beginning of my first session with a woman in her fifties, she asked me how old I was. After I answered, she immediately followed up by saying, "Do you really think you can help me?"

Many clients prefer to see someone who is their same age or older, equating age with wisdom. On the other hand, many families calling to schedule therapy for their teenager are looking for a young therapist, one who can relate to their adolescent child.

In some cases, you may wish to work with someone of your same race or who is also an ethnic or racial minority; this might be true if your therapy concerns involve issues surrounding race and experiences of discrimination.

Many people in the LGBTQ+ community prefer to work with a therapist who is also LGBTQ+ or an ally of the community.

Clients with disabilities may prefer to see a therapist who has special training in issues specific to individuals living with disabilities.

Working with someone who is both accepting of and knowledgeable about your life experience and your community can make a big difference. For some clients, the identity of the therapist is an important consideration, while for others, it may not matter at all. What all clients want, however, is for their therapist to have the capacity to understand their experience and to do so with respect and care.

Graduate programs in counseling require training in multicultural sensitivity. And thankfully (although arguably not soon enough), many white therapists have recently taken extra steps to identify and address implicit bias and systemic racism. Black Lives Matter and other social justice movements have made the work of addressing racism a higher priority for the mental health community as a whole.

Given that mental health professionals are influential to those they serve, professional therapists have a responsibility to constantly self-reflect and self-correct. Nowhere is this more pressing than in the domain of cultural sensitivity. Being able to effectively and respectfully discuss race, gender, sexual orientation, and the politics of power is a skill that all therapists need to have.

CHOOSING A THERAPIST YOU FEEL COMFORTABLE WITH

Now let's look at the variable that makes the biggest difference: personality. Both empirical research and anecdotal reports from clients consistently show that what matters most in therapeutic experiences are the personal characteristics of the therapist. Effective therapists are good listeners, keen observers, open-minded, warm, compassionate, curious, flexible, and committed to ongoing professional development. So how do you find such a person?

Once you have narrowed your search to a few therapists, it is time to reach out and make contact. Start by calling or emailing your prospective therapists with your questions in mind. Asking question can help you get a feel for how the therapist interacts with you. Make no mistake, you are interviewing them. Therapy requires trust, courage, and vulnerability. It is important to choose someone you feel comfortable hiring as your guide for this important journey.

If you don't feel like the first therapist you speak to is a perfect match, don't worry. Talking to multiple therapists before you find the right match is common—so common, in fact, that you'll often see it depicted in film.

In the movie *Stranger Than Fiction*, the protagonist, Harold Crick, suffering from troubling psychological symptoms, sees two therapists before finally choosing the person he feels comfortable working with. In the first case, the provider was a terrible match of personality—and arguably incompetent. In the second case, Harold and his therapist could not agree upon the nature of his problem; she did, however, provide him with a referral to someone who ultimately helped Harold tremendously (an eccentric English professor with an encyclopedic knowledge of literature). The movie is a wonderful illustration of one man's journey of personal transformation, not to mention a terribly funny and heart-warming film.

Harold's initial experience of looking for a therapist is not uncommon. The movie *Good Will Hunting* also begins with a similar sequence of events, highlighting the false starts that can occur when you don't make a connection with the first therapist you see.

So be patient and be prepared to shop around. Taking time to find someone you feel comfortable with is worth the extra effort. ***The relationship between you and your therapist is the most crucial ingredient in the success of your mental health care.***

CHANGING THERAPISTS

In some instances, you may find that the therapist you are seeing is not a good fit. Perhaps you don't feel comfortable with their personality, or maybe their style of therapy isn't working for you. Whatever the reason, it is not unusual to change therapists before your therapy journey is complete.

If you have given your therapist a chance (I typically suggest five sessions to get a feel for someone) and it just isn't working, then don't hesitate to move on. Not all clients and therapists are a match for each other. If you have come to this conclusion, don't worry about hurting your therapist's feelings. This decision is about you, not them.

In moving forward, you do not owe your current therapist an apology or an explanation. It is, of course, considerate to let them know you no longer wish to continue in therapy with them. All you need to do is simply inform your therapist that you will not be continuing in therapy with them. Any further explanation is yours to give, only if you so desire.

Pro Tip: Take Your Time before Committing

I recommend meeting with two or three different therapists for an initial consultation. Once you have selected the person you feel most comfortable with, consider attending approximately five sessions before making your final decision. There are, however, exceptions to these guidelines. You may hit the bull's-eye with the first person you contact. There is no need to look further if you have a good connection from the start.

On the other hand, there is no reason to suffer through the five session rule if you determine that you do not like or trust the therapist you have chosen. What is most important is to never give up! It is common for people to see multiple therapists over the course of their lives. If you aren't getting what you need after a reasonable period of time, move on. And don't worry about hurting your therapist's feelings. That is not a reason to continue working with someone when you aren't getting the help that you need.

CHOOSING THE APPROPRIATE LEVEL OF CARE

As you prepare to begin your mental health journey, it's important to think about a concept known as level of care. For the majority of readers, your issues can be appropriately addressed by outpatient counseling. If, however, you are suffering from an acute addiction, or severe mental illness, a higher level of care will be required. Examples of higher levels of care include in-patient treatment, residential treatment, intensive outpatient (IOP), or some other combination of therapies designed to effectively address your mental health needs. When in doubt, ask prospective therapists for their recommendations regarding the appropriate level of care for you.

Chapter Three

What to Expect from Therapy

If you are new to counseling—or if you have had negative experiences with therapy in the past—this chapter is just for you. I will walk you through each step of the journey of therapy, from start to finish, describing what happens in a typical, satisfactory therapy experience.

INITIAL CONTACT WITH A THERAPIST

Initial contact with a potential therapist will typically occur via phone or email. This first point of contact is a two-way interview. During this encounter, the therapist will gather information about you and your reasons for seeking therapy. This conversation is also an important opportunity for you to gather information about the therapist and, more importantly, to get a feel for their personality.

Ask lots of questions. Where did they go to school? What was their professional training like? How long have they been in practice? How would they address your specific problem or situation? How do they describe their counseling style?

Asking questions will not only provide you with concrete information, it will also give you a sense of how the therapist relates to you. If both you and the therapist decide to set up an initial meeting, an appointment will be made.

Pro Tip: Ask about Their Therapeutic Journey

You can also ask if the therapist has ever been in therapy themselves. I would never see a therapist who hasn't been in therapy. Would you embark upon a backcountry expedition with a guide who hasn't spent any time in the wilderness?

On the other hand, if the therapist starts spilling their guts about their long history of emotional problems, run for the hills! This is a sign that they are not a true professional. A small amount of self-disclosure can be appropriate; excessive sharing that places a burden on you is a red flag.

YOUR FIRST THERAPY APPOINTMENT

Your first therapy appointment will most likely be different from subsequent meetings. During this initial consultation, the therapist will typically ask you a lot of questions—questions about your personal history, your current relationships, your substance use, your health history (both physical and mental health), why you are seeking therapy, and anything else that is connected to your reason for seeking mental health care.

It's not unusual to feel emotionally overwhelmed or drained after the initial meeting; this kind of feeling is normal. It is, however, necessary for the therapist to gather a lot of information in order to know how best to help you.

If you feel nervous about disclosing this much personal information, know that there is no reason to be concerned. Therapists are legally and ethically bound to maintain strict confidentiality. The only exceptions to this rule come into play if there are legitimate concerns of imminent danger to self or others, or if there is suspicion of abuse of a minor or vulnerable adult. Otherwise, you should assume anything you tell them will not be repeated to anyone else, for any reason.

In some cases, your therapist may jump right into therapy in the first session. This approach is also effective. Milton Erickson (a legendary psychiatrist and hypnotherapist who influenced an entire generation of clinicians) would often provide astonishing, unorthodox interventions on his first session, followed up by elaborate homework assignments that often led his patients to a rapid recovery.

During my very first psychotherapy session, my therapist had me do an empty chair exercise in which I had a "conversation" with two conflicted parts of my personality. It was quite helpful.

Under certain circumstances, after the conclusion of the initial consultation, the therapist or client may decide not to move forward with therapy. This can happen for one of two reasons. The therapist may determine that they are not an appropriate fit. If this is the case, you can expect to receive a referral to another therapist who will likely be more able to fulfill your needs. If at all possible, try not to take this decision personally and move forward with the referrals provided.

The second reason for not rescheduling would be that you did not feel comfortable with the therapist. In that case, you owe the therapist neither apology nor explanation. Simply continue your search for another clinician to work with.

PAYING FOR THERAPY

The financial cost of therapy is important to consider. Therapy can be a major investment of both time and money. Variables such as your insurance coverage and what clinician you work with will ultimately determine how much therapy will cost you.

Thanks to the Affordable Care Act, insurance companies are required to cover mental health care. That being said, insurance plans vary widely—both among companies and from state to state. Some plans will cover 100 percent of the cost of therapy, while others leave you responsible for the costs until your annual deductible is met. In most cases, you will be responsible for a copayment for each session, much like any visit to a medical professional. Copays typically range from $10 to $50 per session.

Some therapists do not take insurance, and, likewise, some clients prefer not to use their insurance for psychotherapy. If that is the case, you will need to pay out of pocket. Some therapists offer a sliding scale, based upon your financial means; others have a flat rate.

According to 2021 statistics, the average cost for a psychotherapy session in the United States is $90 per session, with most Americans paying between $60 and $120 per session. These rates typically vary based upon location as well as the experience level of the clinician. It would not be unusual to pay upward of $200 for a fifty-minute session in New York or Los Angeles.

Pro Tip: Find a Therapist Who Is Building Their Practice

If you are paying out of pocket and looking to save a buck, you might consider working with a therapist who is new to private practice. Just because a clinician is less experienced does not necessarily mean they will be less effective, and in many cases, they will be willing to offer reduced fees as they build their practice.

THE PROCESS OF THERAPY

Follow-up sessions are typically different from the initial meeting. Therapy sessions are more dynamic and interactive, with the therapist asking exploratory questions, providing empathy, offering feedback, and, at times, making direct suggestions. Therapeutic styles vary widely as a result of differences in personality, training, and theoretical orientation. Over time, you will likely determine what therapy style works best for you.

The beginning of therapy involves three primary tasks: (1) building a working alliance, including the development of trust and rapport, (2) making a thorough assessment of your needs and goals, and (3) developing and implementing a treatment plan for addressing your mental health concerns and other therapy goals. This process typically takes multiple sessions.

In many cases, your problem might improve rather quickly. It is also common that things will feel worse before they feel better. While this may sound like bad news, do not despair. The reality is that most of us rely on unhealthy coping skills and unconscious defense mechanisms to keep distressing emotions at bay. We compartmentalize, minimize, and repress. We avoid our feelings through obsessions and addictions. We distract ourselves by consuming media and focusing on the ups and downs of others around us.

Therapy, when it is done correctly, shines a light on these patterns of avoidance. Feeling difficult emotions, talking about painful experiences, being open about insecurities is not for the faint of heart. But do not fear. A skilled therapist will provide guidance and support, helping you to pace this process so that it is not overwhelming. They can also teach you new, more effective coping and self-care skills.

The middle of therapy is, well, hard to identify, as we often do not know when therapy will end. That being said, there is often a plateau in the process. This could occur after several weeks or several months. Perhaps you and your therapist have gotten very comfortable with each other, and your initial problems have either resolved or simmered down.

Somewhere along the way, you and your therapist decided that long-term work would help you to arrive at a more robust resolution of your issues, to get to the root of your problems. And so there may be some sessions that are slower than others; from time to time, you may have even forgotten what you were working on for a brief moment. Furthermore, your life may quiet down, leaving you with less to discuss from the day-to-day challenges. And yet, you still may enjoy, and even benefit from, having a standing appointment with a therapist.

HOW LONG WILL THERAPY LAST?

A number of factors influence the length that a course of treatment will take, including these:

- Your reasons for being in therapy
- The nature and severity of the problem
- The theoretical orientation of your therapist
- How quickly you make progress toward your goals
- If you decide to pursue new goals along the way

In some cases, your therapist can reliably predict how long therapy might last within the first few sessions. It is also fairly common that the duration of therapy is unpredictable, even to a seasoned clinician. As a result, it helps to begin therapy with an open mind, especially with regard to the length of the process.

Pro Tip: Different Therapy Techniques Lead to Different Time Frames

Therapists trained in psychodynamic therapy tend to provide long-term therapy (think in terms of years). Therapists trained in cognitive behavioral therapy (CBT) and solution-oriented therapies tend to work in shorter time frames. It helps to keep this in mind when managing your expectations about how long therapy will last with any given provider.

THREE FORMS OF THERAPY

Over the course of my career, I have found that therapy usually follows one of three paths: *solution-oriented, insight-oriented*, or *supportive.*

Solution-oriented therapy is typically short term and can frequently be accomplished in less than six months—sometimes in as few as five to ten sessions. With this kind of brief therapy, the focus is typically a combination of

- Symptom reduction,
- Identification of resources, and
- Strategic solutions.

This form of therapy is often directive, with a focus on the present and the future. Once your presenting problem has been resolved, therapy will come to an end. This type of therapy is ideal for quickly resolving certain situational problems, minor interpersonal conflicts, and other mild-to-moderate concerns.

Insight-oriented, long-term therapy typically takes a minimum of one year and can go on for much longer, depending upon the nature of the problem and the stamina of the client. Long-term therapy can include many of the components of short-term therapy (problem solving, skills building, symptom reduction), but it also seeks to address the underlying causes of problems.

Long-term therapy is concerned with your past, present, and future. This deeper form of therapy is ideal for

- Addressing and resolving the after-effects of trauma,
- Transforming relationship patterns,
- Transforming one's attitudes toward Self and others,
- Developing psychological insight and emotional fluency,
- Addressing existential questions of purpose and meaning, and/or
- Finding greater knowledge of the Self.

Long-term therapy requires a significant commitment of time, money, and energy. It also requires a tolerance for less structure. Some sessions are exploratory in nature and do not yield immediate results. Long-term therapy also requires a strong and trusting relationship with your therapist. People who have a positive experience with long-term therapy often report the experience to be transformative and life changing.

The third form, **supportive counseling**, can be either short term or long term. What makes supportive counseling unique is that the presenting problem is related to an ongoing stressor due to circumstances outside of your control. Some common examples of issues that would require supportive therapy are

- Managing a chronic mental illness,
- Grief and loss following the death of a loved one,
- Adjustment to a medical diagnosis or significant change in health status, or
- Caregiver stress related to a loved one's health problems and needs.

This type of therapy can at times be both solution-oriented and depth-oriented, but is most often geared toward providing ongoing emotional support.

No matter what form of therapy you need, you can take steps to get the best possible outcome. In upcoming chapters, I will explore ways you can get the most out of your therapy, as well as how and when to draw your therapy to a close.

Chapter Four

Client Participation Is Required

Effective therapy is the result of a synergy between client and counselor. Of course, choosing a skilled therapist, especially someone you groove with, is a big part of the equation. But did you know that you play a crucial role as well?

Yes, you have a responsibility to your own therapy. Your attitude, expectations, honesty, motivation, and gumption—how you show up in each session—all make a difference. As Will Rogers once said, "Even though you are on the right track, you will get run over if you just sit there." In this chapter, we will roll up our sleeves and dig into things you can do to get the most from your therapy journey.

CLEAR GOALS WITH AN ASTERISK

When you begin therapy, it is helpful to identify goals. These goals can be simple and direct—for example, you may want to get sober, overcome depression, develop better self-care, or improve your relationships. Or perhaps you are looking for guidance with career development, or maybe you need assistance with making an important decision in your life. Goals can also be open-ended—for example, you may go into therapy in order to better understand yourself.

In most cases, your goals will flow naturally from your reason for going into therapy. If you call a therapist because you are suffering from anxiety, your goals will include a decrease in the frequency and intensity of anxiety attacks. But even if this is the case, and your goals seem obvious, I strongly encourage you to take some time to reflect upon what you want from therapy.

One way to go about this is to use your imagination. Picture yourself saying goodbye to your therapist as you wrap up your last session. What's different in your life then? Work backward from there. And while you are at it, give yourself permission to branch out and to go big. Over the course of therapy, you may find yourself generating goals you had not originally considered. Have you left behind dreams or neglected an ambition? Is there a forgotten part of yourself sitting on the shelf just gathering dust? There is no better time than when going into therapy to take inventory of these important questions.

PREPARING FOR EACH SESSION

If therapy goals function as your blueprint, then therapy sessions are the work periods that keep your project moving forward. While your therapist has a responsibility to guide and structure your sessions, how you participate in sessions makes a big difference too.

Therapy is a place for you to talk about anything that's on your mind. You can think of it as a blank canvas, a sacred space, an hour just for you. What a rare gift. However, with such freedom, two main challenges can arise. Some people, whom I'll call under-talkers, freeze up, feeling anxious and unsure, with nothing to say. Other people, the over-talkers, might find themselves flooded with too many ideas and topics to discuss, leaving little time for the therapist to respond.

A skilled therapist will be able to provide structure, offering direction to both the anxious under-talker as well as the chatty over-talker. But even with the guidance of a skilled therapist, it can be helpful for you to come to your session with topics in mind and appropriate expectations.

Whether you are an over-talker, an under-talker, or somewhere in between, it can be beneficial to take time before each session to think about what you want to discuss. I recommend setting aside time before each session to both reflect and then make a list of specific topics and experiences to address.

Pro Tip: Write Notes throughout the Week

Many clients find it helpful to make notes throughout the week between sessions. We often forget thoughts or feelings after the intensity of the moment fades. That's why it really helps to get in a habit of writing down observations and significant experiences before your next session, while they are still fresh. As a bonus, when you get in the habit of making notes in advance of your sessions, you will be sure to bring your notebook with you to counseling. As a result, you can take your journey to the next level by writing down insights that come up during your therapy sessions.

VENTING: IT'S NOT THE SAME AS WORKING ON YOUR ISSUES

In addition to keeping your goals in mind, it's also important to think about the distinction between venting about stressful life events and working on your issues.

This is not to say that there's no place for venting in therapy. More than likely, there will come a time when you want to flop down on your therapist's couch to unload complaints and vent frustrations. If, however, each and every therapy session turns into a habitual replay of the events from your week, if therapy becomes a complaint ritual focusing on the same old topics, then something important is missing.

It is quite possible for a person to spend months, or even years, in therapy focusing entirely on the stressors of daily life, without talking about the issues that truly relate to their personal goals. Though venting can feel good in the moment, if it makes up the majority of your sessions, you're missing out. So, as you consider what topics you'd like to discuss in therapy, keep in mind your goals and consider what really matters at a deeper level. This is how you can do your part to keep your therapy on track.

HONESTY, PRIVACY, AND SECRECY

According to a 2016 study in the *Counselling Psychology Quarterly*, 93 percent of clients reported lying to their therapist at least once. This research revealed that clients are dishonest for the same reasons that people are dishonest in their other relationships: to preserve an image, because they feel ashamed of something, to avoid dealing with difficult issues, and as an artifact of self-deception.

In some cases, clients lie to protect their therapist's feelings; in others, they fear being judged by their therapist. It's also common to lie or omit important information to avoid an issue and preserve one's denial system.

If you find yourself lying in therapy—either directly or by omission—do not fear. This problem is simply an opportunity in disguise. It could indicate the need to further explore the level of trust that you have with your therapist. Or it could mean that you just aren't ready to talk about a particular issue yet.

This brings us to the important distinction between secrecy and privacy. One of the many times I had the privilege of seeing author and therapist Esther Perel lecture about her work with couples, she articulated the difference between the two. A secret represents something shameful, often some form of betrayal (a secret affair, a secret drug problem, secretly spending the family's retirement at the casino). But privacy represents your inner garden—a personal, psychological space.

Sadly, popular psychology has at times been guilty of overlooking the value of privacy, often promoting the notion that psychological health involves telling the people you are close to everything you think, feel, want, and dream about *at all times*.

Sharing deeply with those you love and trust can be a rich, intimacy-building experience. But does emotional vulnerability require that you totally give up your privacy? Is your partner entitled to know every thought that goes through your head?

Should you be obligated to confess to your mate if you have an erotic dream involving someone else? Must you share every detail of every insecurity you have? My answer to these questions is no.

And the same applies to your therapist. Your therapist is not entitled to know any more than you want to share with them. You are allowed privacy, even within the therapeutic relationship. Therapy ultimately depends upon trust and openness; that trust must be built, over time. If, however, you are living behind a wall and unable to share anything meaningful about your inner life, you have most likely taken the concept of privacy too far.

So, if you find yourself lying to your therapist, or contemplating lying to your therapist, take a step back. Ask yourself why you are doing so. Is it because you don't trust this person yet, or because you aren't ready to face this issue? Hopefully, if you have an effective working relationship with your therapist, you can find meaningful things to work on as you build up the trust and courage to be fully honest about all the issues that truly matter. If, on the other hand, you determine that you simply don't trust your therapist at all, perhaps you should consider working with someone else.

COMMON THERAPY MISSTEPS

We've covered big topics like goal setting, preparing for each session, staying on task, and issues of honesty and privacy. But a successful therapy experience also involves getting a handle on smaller issues too.

Let's look at some other common missteps that clients sometimes make:

- Frequently missing or rescheduling appointments
- Consistently arriving late for sessions
- Not thinking about insights between sessions
- Not following through on suggestions from your therapist
- Quitting therapy too soon
- Trying too hard to control the process

- Staying silent when you dislike something your therapist says or does
- Changing therapists too soon
- Waiting too long to change therapists
- Having unrealistic expectations about how fast therapy works
- Having unrealistic expectations about what therapists can do
- Entering therapy with hidden agendas that you don't discuss up front (expecting your therapist to testify in court on your behalf or write a letter to your employer, for example)

Each of these pitfalls represents a way you could potentially get in your own way. Many therapists will confront these kinds of behaviors, but not all will. It's ultimately up to you to do everything within your power to get the most out of your therapy. Just like working with a personal trainer, taking music lessons, or any other endeavor that involves learning skills and facing challenges, your level of dedication and commitment will determine the outcome you will get.

Pro Tip: You Can Ask to Change Appointment Times

If you find that your appointment time is difficult for you to make or somehow makes it harder for you to fully engage with therapy, ask your therapist if you can come at a different day or time. In some cases, this can be a simple way to resolve a problem of frequently missed appointments, frequent tardiness, or not getting the most from your sessions.

PROVIDING YOUR THERAPIST WITH FEEDBACK

It's a good idea to provide feedback to your therapist whenever appropriate. Therapists are human, and they sometimes make mistakes in session. For example, some therapists become very attached to specific theories or techniques. If you find that your therapist is viewing your situation in a way that doesn't make sense to you, or if your therapist uses interventions that you don't find to be helpful, it is important to let them know.

While some readers may naturally feel comfortable making these kinds of direct confrontations, many others may not. In my experience, most clients are reluctant to tell their therapist anything critical, and thus do not provide feedback. But any therapist worth their salt will be able to handle constructive feedback. And while most therapists are very observant, they are not mind readers. The only way they will know if something is bothering you is if you tell them.

One of my favorite therapists was enthusiastic about her clients using a technique that involved prescribed tantrums (pounding a mattress with fists, shouting, and so on). The bulk of our work together was tremendously helpful, but the tantrum technique just wasn't doing it for me. I eventually told her that I was getting a lot out of talking, but the other part of our sessions wasn't really helping. She was understanding and able to adapt.

Similarly, I have had clients confront me when they felt misunderstood or when they disliked a comment I made. The beauty of therapy is that, in many cases, these kinds of confrontations lead to greater closeness between counselor and client, sometimes even to therapeutic breakthroughs. Taking an emotional risk and having your feelings both respected and validated goes a long way.

On the other hand, if you bring up an issue and your therapist becomes defensive or is unwilling to adapt to your request—assuming it is reasonable and respectful—then you have a problem. This unlikely scenario is no reason to avoid giving feedback. Furthermore, studies have shown that the best therapy outcomes arise from therapy relationships where corrections are made early on in the therapeutic endeavor.

There is no right or wrong answer to the question of what you should talk about in therapy. The point is to be thoughtful about how you want to use your hour and to take ownership of what you are working on.

Chapter Five

How Therapy Affects Others in Your Life

Your choice to pursue therapy will not only affect you, it can also have an effect on the important people in your life. In this chapter, we will explore the ways in which your therapy journey can impact those around you. We will also take a look at the thorny issue of what to do if someone in your life is opposed to your getting help.

TO SHARE OR NOT TO SHARE

As we established in the last chapter, the right to privacy is an important one. Your decision to receive mental health care is yours to keep to yourself or yours to share with the world. Personally, I'm very grateful that the stigma around mental health issues continues to decrease. More and more people—both celebrities and everyday individuals alike—are opening up about their mental health struggles, including their decision to get help.

If you feel happy or proud that you are getting counseling, share the good news with others. If you prefer to keep the decision to yourself, that's okay too. I have many clients who fall on either side of this spectrum.

THE DOMINO EFFECT

According to systems theory, the whole is greater than the sum of its parts. As a result, when one member of a system—a couple or a family, for example—makes changes, it will necessarily have an effect on the rest of the system. Thus, even if your reasons for being in therapy are not specifically focused on relationship issues, the changes you experience as a consequence of being in therapy will most likely have an impact on the key people in your life.

Keeping this domino effect in mind, along with the willingness to talk about it with those in your family or inner circle, is a good idea.

OPPOSITION TO THERAPY

While many people in your life are likely to be supportive of your decision to get help, some individuals will feel threatened by your foray into the territory of self-reflection and personal changes.

In my experience, those hostile to therapy fall into two categories: (1) people who have a significant backlog of unresolved trauma and, as a result, feel threatened by the notion of digging into the past, and (2) people in your life who are mistreating you. Anyone who is abusing or neglecting you will instinctively know that, sooner or later, you may tell your therapist about the ways you have been harmed by them, and that ultimately the relationship could be in jeopardy.

If you have a parent, sibling, friend, or spouse who is actively hostile toward your endeavor of personal transformation, then you may need to behave strategically. The truth is, if someone in your life is opposed to your getting help, what more do you need to know?

Chapter Six

Therapy Timelines

What does a typical progression of therapy look like? How do you know when it's time for your therapy to conclude? Can you resume therapy after you have stopped? This chapter explores these common questions.

HOW OFTEN WILL YOU MEET WITH YOUR THERAPIST

In many cases, therapy will begin with a standing appointment, the frequency of which will be determined by your needs. The majority of the time, your therapy will start with weekly sessions or, in some cases, sessions every other week. In the occasion of severe and acute problems, your therapist may recommend that you come in twice a week until stabilization has occurred.

This initial schedule can go on for quite a while; over time, once your concerns begin to improve, your therapist will likely recommend that you transition to less frequent appointments. This second phase of therapy—typically every other week—can also go on for quite some time as well. During this second phase, you will be able to continue working on your goals as well as deepen insights and changes made thus far.

Finally, once your treatment goals are met, your therapist will likely recommend one of three options: (1) monthly maintenance appointments, (2) appointments as needed, or (3) termination of therapy.

This is a typical progression of therapy, but there are of course many possible exceptions to the rule. This process can last anywhere from just a few months to several years. The duration of therapy ultimately depends on multiple factors, including your goals, the nature of your problem, and the theoretical orientation of your therapist.

WHEN AND HOW TO END

Given all that can transpire during a course of therapy, how do you know when it's time to stop?

The simple truth is you can stop at any time that you want. Another way to decide is, if your goals have been met, and you do not have new goals to explore, it may be time. A general rule that I often use with my clients is that if we have three sessions in a row with no issues to address (we end up spending the entire session talking about music, movies, travel, or sports), that is a clear indication it is time to draw therapy to a close.

Either you or your therapist can suggest an end to therapy. Your therapist may recommend that therapy draw to a close if it is their opinion that you are ready. On the other hand, if you feel ready to stop, all you need to do is let your therapist know.

If you are the one proposing termination, however, know that there are some instances in which your therapist may encourage you to continue. This is often the case when you confuse the resolution of an immediate symptom with the resolution of the underlying issue. In such a scenario, your therapist may recommend that you continue with therapy until more work has been done to address the root causes of your problem or concern. It is, of course, ultimately your decision, and you are always free to stop.

Once you have decided to end therapy, your last session may involve reflection upon the work that you have done together, including a review of progress made. Having established a therapeutic relationship, many therapists have a policy of allowing former clients to easily return for either a single session "tune-up" or to resume ongoing therapy services. This is a topic worth discussing with your therapist if you are considering taking a break from therapy.

THERAPY CAN INVOLVE MANY CHAPTERS

Your therapy journey may well contain multiple chapters, or *episodes of care*. I frequently have former clients return and do another round of counseling with me. Having resolved your original problem, you may be ready to stop seeing your therapist. Years later, you may decide that you want to return to therapy. This can happen for a number of reasons:

- The original problem came back.
- New issues or life stressors have emerged.
- You want to engage in deeper exploration of the Self.

Whatever the reason, having developed a positive relationship with your therapist, you can easily continue your journey with them. Or perhaps you will feel drawn to work with someone new, to gain a different set of tools and perspectives on your situation. While each person's situation is unique, it is common for therapy to involve multiple episodes, over the course of time.

So far, we have explored what you can expect from a positive therapy experience, including many of the practical nuts and bolts of the therapeutic process. Not all therapy experiences are positive, however. In the next chapter we will discuss what happens when therapy goes awry, including practical solutions you can take to get your therapy back on track.

Chapter Seven

What's Not Supposed to Happen in Therapy

Sometimes, therapy goes off the rails. I've heard more stories than I can count about people's bad experiences in counseling. I am always disheartened by them. Sadly, negative experiences on the therapy couch can discourage you from trying therapy again. The sooner you can determine that there is a problem, however, the sooner you can move on and find a better therapist, thus saving yourself precious time and resources.

If you're unsure about whether your own therapy experience is appropriate, read on for information on some things that are not supposed to happen when you are getting professional help.

BOUNDARY CROSSING

Some therapists are dangerous. Your therapist is responsible for maintaining certain fundamental boundaries at all times. It is their job to clearly define and reinforce the professional nature of the therapeutic relationship. The most critical boundaries are those that prohibit engaging in romantic or sexual relationships with clients.

When this boundary is crossed, there is a great risk of serious psychological harm to clients. Other forms of boundary violations include engaging in other forms of detrimental relationships with clients outside of the office.

Thankfully, these kinds of boundary violations are rare. The overwhelming majority of practicing therapists never cross these boundaries. But just like in any profession, there are always a few bad apples who use their position of power for personal gain, with no remorse about the harm they cause to others.

Therapists must also maintain other boundaries such as protecting patient confidentiality and handling any contact outside of sessions appropriately and with professionalism. For example, you and your therapist might have children that go to the same school, or you may have some other social overlap. Effective therapists know how to maintain healthy boundaries in all aspects of the therapeutic relationship. The healing power of psychotherapy depends in large part on the feeling of safety that is created by clearly defined boundaries.

Your therapist is responsible for creating a container for your healing work. This includes the physical space of their office, the time boundaries around each session, clear expectations about how much (if any) communication will occur outside of session, and any other aspect of the therapeutic relationship.

When you know that your therapist is creating and maintaining appropriate, strong borders around the relationship, it becomes easier to relax and let your guard down—which is necessary to obtain a good result from therapy.

LACK OF PROFESSIONALISM

Some therapists aren't very grown up. Just as therapists must maintain appropriate boundaries, they must also conduct themselves in a professional manner during your time together.

This doesn't mean that therapists have to act in a specific, prescribed way. Therapists, just like everyone else, have a wide variety of personality types. Many will utilize humor, liberally use four letter words, and share entertaining stories to prove a point. Others are more formal and reserved. As a matter of fact, it's a good thing that therapists are a diverse bunch; how better to connect with the diverse clients they serve? While one person may relate well to a therapist who has a formal relationship style, someone else will prefer a therapist who is more casual in how they relate. These personality differences can enhance rapport, thus increasing client engagement.

While a therapist with a colorful personality is not a problem, one who engages in excessive self-disclosure is. If your therapist shares too much information about themselves, that is a red flag.

A small amount of self-disclosure for the purpose of making a personal connection or to make a point is considered clinically appropriate and is a normal part of therapy. Appropriate sharing will typically (1) last less than five minutes, (2) be in some way connected to your concerns, and (3) be presented in a way that you don't feel burdened. In other words, you should not feel that your therapist is looking for emotional support from you.

On the other hand, if your therapist talks about themselves excessively, if their sharing is not designed to help you, or if their sharing simply makes you feel uncomfortable, there is a problem. If you find yourself getting confused about who is the therapist and who is the client, it's time to head for the door.

LACK OF ENGAGEMENT

Some therapists are phoning it in. They may have good boundaries and behave in a professional manner, and yet you get the feeling that they are not present, not paying close attention, or just don't care.

This lack of engagement could be caused by any number or reasons—professional burnout, being in the wrong profession, being distracted by a personal crisis. But regardless of the reason, you get the feeling that your concerns are just not that important to your therapist.

If this is the case, it may be time to look elsewhere. After all, if you're showing up and giving a full commitment to working on yourself, you have the right to expect your therapist to bring their A game as well. For your time together, you should expect 100 percent of their attention and resourcefulness.

LACK OF DIRECTION AND STRUCTURE

Some therapists simply aren't effective. They might have a kind heart and a genuine desire to help, but their therapy lacks direction.

This can be a subtle point. There are many legitimate, effective forms of therapy (psychoanalysis and client-centered therapy, to name two) that are nondirective. With these forms of treatment, the therapist will ask open-ended questions and follow the client's lead. These approaches can have a meandering quality, and some sessions may feel unstructured. The overall treatment plan, however, is guided by sound theories and does have a clinical strategy designed to help you reach your goals.

On the other hand, some therapists are not grounded in a strong theoretical foundation, and, thus, the therapy lacks adequate structure and direction.

If you suspect that your sessions are leading you on a journey to nowhere, don't be afraid to ask your therapist some hard questions. What is their treatment plan? What theoretical orientation and/or clinical strategies are they drawing on? How do they view your problem and your goals? What is their plan to help you get where you want to go? You may be pleasantly surprised by the answer. On the other hand, if your therapist looks like a deer in the headlights when you ask the hard questions, it may be time to find someone new to work with.

PREMATURE TERMINATION

Some therapists resist going deep. Many clinicians practicing today are trained in cognitive behavioral therapy or other similar modalities geared toward symptom reduction through short-term care. And while CBT is very effective, it is not a one-size-fits-all solution.

Too many times I have known clients who have finally gotten the nerve to get into therapy and made a connection with a therapist, only to be prematurely discharged from treatment as soon as their initial symptoms resolved.

Now, don't get me wrong. Long-term, depth-oriented psychotherapy is certainly not for everyone. The great Milton

Erickson and the many expert therapists who are a part of his lineage have proven that tremendous changes can occur from brief therapy. Short-term, strategic therapy certainly has its place.

The problem I wish to address here are those occasions when a therapist misses an opportunity to help a client who is motivated to do deep work. It's not unusual for someone to seek therapy due to depression, anxiety, or a relationship problem, only to discover a deeper longing to know themselves better. If, however, your therapist recommends a premature end to therapy, the chance to go deeper, to explore past hurts, and to ultimately engage in a longer, more meaningful journey of analysis and self-discovery will have been lost.

This longer process is the original foundation of psychotherapy. Sadly, many therapists today are not properly trained in the core elements of analytical therapy and thus may not be comfortable going beyond the original problem toward a deeper exploration of the psyche.

Pro Tip: Let Your Therapist Know If You Want to Keep Going

If you want to keep going while your therapist is trying to wrap things up, don't hesitate to speak your mind. You may have to move on and find a therapist who is more comfortable with long-term depth-oriented therapy, or you may just be able to talk your current therapist into going deeper.

It is my sincere hope that you will not run into any of these problems on your psychotherapy journey. If, however, you do encounter any of these pitfalls, don't wait to take action and course correct. If your therapist has done something egregious, you should consider reporting them to their licensing board. In less severe cases, however, you may simply need to move on and find a new therapist to work with.

PART II

The Journey

"It's easier to put on a pair of shoes
than wrap the earth in leather."

—Chögyam Trungpa, Tibetan Buddhist teacher

Chapter Eight

Maps and Guidance: Finding Direction in Unfamiliar Terrain

When embarking on a journey into unfamiliar territory, having a good map with you can make all the difference. This chapter is designed to keep you on course as you pursue your mental health goals.

In practical terms, this involves beginning with an accurate and thorough assessment that will guide the direction of your therapy toward the correct sequence of steps. While it is your therapist's job to make an assessment of your mental health needs, the more you know, the better off you will be. Here are the three categories that guide my decision-making for my clients, including related concepts for your consideration.

BIOLOGICAL FACTORS

First and foremost, we are biological creatures. The state of your physical body has a tremendous impact on your perceptions and emotions. As a result, when you map your journey toward greater health, first address all possible biological contributions to your problem.

Are you getting enough sleep? Sleep deprivation wreaks havoc on both mind and body, causing a host of cognitive and emotional problems. Irritability, poor concentration, memory trouble, and depressed mood are all associated with sleep debt. In his book *Why We Sleep*, sleep and dream researcher Matthew Walker makes a compelling case for getting a full night of sleep every night. If there were a drug that gave you all the benefits that regular, quality sleep provides, people would pay big bucks for it. But it's available to you, for free. It's called restorative sleep.

Are you eating well? Are you moving your body and staying active? Inadequate nutrition and insufficient exercise can also negatively affect your mental health.

When was your last physical? It is always a good idea to schedule a physical examination with a primary care provider to rule out any medical problems that could be contributing to psychological symptoms. For example, a thyroid imbalance is a common medical condition that can cause psychiatric symptoms such as anxiety, depression, irritability, and fatigue.

Another common biological cause of mental illness is genetics. Individuals who suffer from schizophrenia, bipolar disorder, obsessive-compulsive disorder, ADHD, and some forms of recurrent depression typically have an inherited imbalance in key neurotransmitters as well as structural differences in specific regions of the brain. These neurological conditions are thought to be genetically transmitted.

If you suffer from any of these conditions, you will most likely need psychiatric medication in order to experience relief. If you suspect that you may have one of the ailments listed above, schedule a consultation with a psychiatric provider. Once a diagnosis has been made and a proper regimen of medication therapy has been established, psychotherapy then becomes an essential component of your treatment plan.

You may find it interesting to know that just like psychotherapy, the field of psychiatry continues to evolve. Many of today's psychiatrists deliver patient care with a holistic approach, drawing upon a wide range of treatment options to help their patients thrive.

In addition to new medication offerings, there are promising advances in the use of ECT (electroconvulsive therapy), TMS (transcranial magnetic stimulation), and intravenous ketamine infusions; these three treatments are proving to be effective for individuals with treatment-resistant depression.

With highly promising clinical trials under way, the next frontier of psychiatric medicine is the therapeutic application of psychedelic drugs. A renaissance in research on therapist-assisted psychedelic sessions is producing encouraging results. Current studies include the use of MDMA (a drug commonly known as ecstasy) for the treatment of PTSD (posttraumatic stress disorder), and psilocybin mushrooms for the treatment of depression, anxiety, and addictions.

No matter what your mental health issues are, keeping in mind the needs of the body is crucial.

SITUATIONAL FACTORS

Unexpected challenges are a part of life. Even for the gritty and resilient, life can sometimes become overwhelming. This is especially true when multiple problems stack on top of each other. When this happens, it can take a toll on your psychological well-being.

Examples of situational factors that can impact your mental health include illness, chronic pain, relocation, job change, job loss, break-ups, divorce, family conflict, miscarriage, the birth of a child, the death of a loved one, children leaving home, retirement, political instability, and chaotic environmental factors. Situational factors can be either transient or chronic. Whatever your situation, therapy for situational stressors involves a combination of solution-oriented strategies and emotional support.

A phenomenon I have seen many times in my practice goes like this: A client is faced with formidable situational stressors that in turn awaken and amplify preexisting emotional issues. For example, a combination of problems at home and work sends the client into an episode of depression and anxiety. In the midst of this turmoil, the client comes face-to-face with unresolved emotional issues from the past.

If anything like this is happening to you, a skillful therapist will help you get through your present crisis, while also encouraging growth and insight along the way. As a result, there is the potential for you to emerge from your crisis a stronger, more self-aware person. It is a form of wisdom to see a crisis as an opportunity for growth.

For some people who experience a situational crisis, therapy is a short-term endeavor, concluding once the crisis is resolved. For others, short-term therapy opens the door to a longer, deeper journey of psychological change. Here is an old Taoist story that illustrates that concept of hardship as opportunity:

> There was once an old farmer who had worked his crops for many years. One day his horse ran away. Upon hearing the news, his neighbors came to visit.
>
> "Such bad luck," they said sympathetically.
>
> "Maybe," the farmer replied.
>
> The next morning the horse returned, bringing with it two other wild horses.
>
> "Such good luck!" the neighbors exclaimed.
>
> "Maybe," replied the old man.
>
> The following day, his son tried to ride one of the untamed horses, was thrown, and broke his leg. Again, the neighbors came to offer their sympathy on his misfortune.
>
> "Such bad luck," they said.
>
> "Maybe," answered the farmer.
>
> The day after, military officials came to the village to draft young men into the army. Seeing that the son's leg was broken, they passed him by.
>
> "Such good luck!" cried the neighbors.
>
> "Maybe," said the farmer.

PSYCHOLOGICAL FACTORS

Emotional injuries that never fully healed, neglected aspects of the Self, stifled creativity, unfulfilled purpose, identity confusion, recurrent dreams begging for attention—these are the true concerns of the psyche.

Underneath the daily stressors described earlier, each of us has an interior landscape of rich experience that profoundly shapes our emotional lives, that influences our important decisions, and that ultimately determines the quality of our relationships with others. These are all examples of psychological factors that lead a person to pursue therapy.

In most cases, these issues will make themselves known through symptoms: unwanted thoughts, feelings, and behaviors that cause distress and interfere with your quality of life. The most common symptoms people experience are anxiety, depression, guilt, self-critical thoughts, perfectionism, feeling numb, chronic tiredness, and confusion. Symptoms can occur together or in isolation.

More often than not, psychological symptoms have their origins in negative experiences with caregivers during childhood, as well as unresolved traumatic experiences that can occur any time during a lifetime. If you suffer from one or more of these psychological symptoms, it may help to talk to your therapist about healing past trauma, uncovering repressed emotions, and exploring unfulfilled purpose.

MOVING FORWARD

The lion's share of this book is concerned with exploring the psychological factors that contribute to mental health problems. In my experience, people are drawn to therapy by a deep desire to heal, grow, and realize their full potential.

The personal crises and dreadful symptoms that motivate us to get help are the alarm bells of the psyche, begging us to wake up and to discover and express who we truly are. The remainder of this part of the book offers multiple ideas and practices designed to help you to both understand and transform psychological suffering.

Chapter Nine

Travel Gear: Get Outfitted for the Journey Ahead

Alfred Wainwright, the famous British long-distance hiker, explorer, and guidebook author, once said, "There's no such thing as bad weather, only unsuitable clothing." And while climate change has undoubtably brought us bad weather, Wainwright's message is nonetheless salient. Bad weather and suitable clothing represent two very different mindsets.

The ability to pivot from one mindset to another, to reframe a problem such that new perspectives and novel solutions can be seen, is at the heart of therapeutic change. Moving from a bad weather mentality to the search for suitable clothing is the goal.

As you make your psychotherapy journey, you will be loading up your metaphorical backpack with the gear you need to support yourself along the way. This "gear" falls into two categories: (1) attitudes you bring to the process, and (2) tools, techniques, and skills your therapist provides. There is no one-size-fits-all technique for psychological growth.

While some people will find meditation tremendously helpful, others will find they just can't stick with it. And while cognitive behavioral therapy fits like a glove for some clients, for others it may be too dry. Consider me as your ambassador to the wide world of ideas and techniques within the self-help marketplace. My hope is to introduce you to a variety of tools and give you an idea of what's available to you.

COGNITIVE BEHAVIORAL APPROACHES

Cognitive behavioral therapy (known widely by its acronym CBT) has become a rather large tent over the years, one that offers a host of solution-oriented strategies for addressing a wide array of mental health concerns. Originally developed by Aaron Beck and Albert Ellis in the 1960s and 1970s, its roots can be found in the philosophical tradition of Stoicism. Indeed, the notion that logic can be used to identify and uproot false beliefs that lead to psychological suffering harkens back to ancient Greece.

CBT represents one of the many ways that psychotherapy has evolved over time. Its founders, trained in traditional psychoanalysis, discovered the prevalent role that distorted thinking patterns play in common maladies such as depression, anxiety, and poor self-esteem. Some therapists provide formal CBT, which tends to be more structured in approach, while many other practitioners blend techniques and concepts from CBT into a more eclectic approach to therapy. Either way, the value in identifying and replacing self-defeating thought patterns with thought patterns that are both empowering and true cannot be understated.

The behavioral side of the equation involves a willingness to try out new things. Some therapists are keen on homework assignments: prescribed activities designed to promote positive change. After all, it's what happens in between your counseling sessions that often makes the most difference. Examples of these behavioral interventions include physical exercise and other forms of self-care.

Another common example of a behavioral approach to therapy are approach behaviors. For example, if you are socially anxious, your therapist might suggest a task of approaching three strangers and asking them for the time before your next session. All too often, we get into the habit of avoiding that which scares us. At first, avoidance provides relief. But over time, patterns of avoidance become a bigger problem than the original object of fear. In extreme cases, it can lead to being permanently homebound. Therapeutic change thus involves gradually approaching the source of your fear, in incremental doses.

MINDFULNESS MEDITATION

People have relied on meditation for both mental stability and spiritual growth since before the time of the Buddha. And while the practice is most heavily associated with Eastern religions, each of the Abrahamic religions lays claim to its own form of contemplative practice, representing Western varieties of meditation.

Meditation gained traction in America in the twentieth century. Two Suzukis—Shunryu Suzuki and D. T. Suzuki—served as ambassadors of Zen Buddhism to the West. Carl Jung, Karen Horney, and Erich Fromm were among the first psychotherapists to integrate insights from Eastern wisdom into their clinical practice.

In the late 1970s, Jon Kabat-Zinn developed Mindfulness-Based Stress Reduction (MBSR) at the University of Massachusetts Medical School. Based in empirical research, MBSR represents an effort to strip away the cultural and religious dimensions of meditation. Approaching mindfulness meditation as a secular endeavor with applications for health care and wellness has made meditation available to a much wider audience. Multiple studies have shown MBSR to be effective in the treatment of stress, anxiety, depression, and other psychological concerns.

Whether you prefer a traditional, spiritual approach or a more modern, clinical approach, meditation practice and other mindfulness exercises are a powerful adjunct to psychotherapy. Books, apps, videos, and meditation groups are all fantastic ways to get started.

THERAPEUTIC WRITING

Journaling and psychotherapy fit together like a hand in a glove. In fact, many of my clients show up to session with a well-worn journal in hand; others carry a brand new diary, ready to capture new insights. Many of my younger clients prefer to make notes on their smartphones. Regardless of format, maintaining a journal of some sort, in session and beyond, can help to capture ideas and feelings when they are fresh.

There are multiple ways to approach therapeutic writing. Journaling involves regular reflection on thoughts, feelings, and significant life events. This can be helpful because sometimes writing about experiences allows us to crystalize insights and approach difficult subjects before we are ready to share them with anyone else. If you are someone who grew up in a home with intrusive parents or if you worry about your journal being read after you are gone, then consider that it's okay to destroy your journal when you are done with it. The point isn't to hang onto your journal forever (unless you want to); it is to be able to express yourself fully and honestly, without fear of your journal being read without your consent.

In addition to traditional journaling, there is the Pennebaker method for processing traumatic memories. James Pennebaker studied the therapeutic effects of expressive writing at the University of Texas at Austin. His approach involves writing about memories and feelings associated with traumatic events, sometimes repeatedly, until the issue begins to lose its emotional charge. This technique has been empirically validated and can help to integrate painful memories.

Julia Cameron, author of *The Artist's Way*, recommends a writing technique called Morning Pages, which involves writing three pages in a stream of consciousness, first thing in the morning. This exercise has been known to help lubricate one's creativity, thus fostering a greater flow of ideas.

TRACKING YOURSELF

Finally, one of my personal favorites is the practice of tracking target behaviors and mood changes for the purpose of better studying specific areas of life. Examples include logging food or alcohol intake, recording the frequency of self-critical thoughts, and tracking changes to your mood.

As you record the target behavior or emotion, you can also keep track of related variables such as sleep, exercise, weather changes, interpersonal encounters, or anything else that might possibly have an effect on the issue at hand.

Tracking is different from journaling in that your goal is simply to record the frequency of behaviors or experiences along with any relevant observations, rather than to dive deep into any thoughts or memories. With behavioral and mood tracking, it helps to utilize the mindset of a scientist—your own behaviors and mental states become the object of your study. This technique has the benefit of bypassing any resistance you may have to making changes, as you start with recording, not reducing.

BODY-CENTERED APPROACHES

When poets write about emotions, they rely on language of the body. From gut feelings to broken hearts, our emotional experiences sometimes go all the way down to the bone. Contemporary trauma researchers are discovering the same truth—our bodies are where emotional memories are stored and released. And while much of psychotherapy is centered around talking, a significant part of the healing process often involves physical movement and release.

Yoga, massage, martial arts, and physical exercise of any kind are all vehicles for achieving greater psychological well-being. Chapter 43 on trauma and PTSD offers more detailed information about the role of physical activities in the resolution of traumatic stress.

Regardless of your issue, it's always a good idea to include the body in your approach to psychological growth. While heady insights can be quite liberating, it's nearly always a good idea to take a walk and let new discoveries settle into the body.

HEALING THROUGH ART

Sometimes, the only sensible thing to do in the wake of loss and pain is to make art. Creative expression of all kinds can become part of your personal healing journey. And before you stop reading, no, you do not have to have artistic talent to tap into the benefits of artistic expression.

The VA at Walter Reed has developed programs designed to help combat veterans heal traumatic brain injuries and PTSD through mask-making. Wounded veterans, many of whom had no prior experience making art, paint masks that illustrate their feelings of both pain and patriotism.

Sometimes the best way to tell your story is with imagery. Visual expression is not for everyone though. Many others have found healing and release through music and dance, tapping into the timeless pulse of life. Theater and performance art can also be powerful vehicles for experimenting with new forms of self-expression. Much like body-centered approaches, art-based activities allow us to express emotions in ways that go beyond words.

UTILIZATION PRINCIPLE

There is a tired phrase that goes something like this—*everything happens for a reason.* Don't get me wrong. If this idea works for you, if it gives you comfort, that's fine. But for many others, it is hollow at best and often hurtful in the face of loss and hardship.

My favorite alternative to this idea is that whatever happens can be worked with and often utilized for good. The utilization principle is credited to Milton Erickson whose extensive writings and teachings on therapy were always grounded in his unshakable belief that whatever a client experienced could be utilized for their healing. And while the principle was originally designed for therapists, clients can use it too.

Perhaps this idea sounds like a fancy derivative of "when life gives you lemons, make lemonade." And while that may be true, I have seen it work, over and over again. Some examples of the utilization principle in practice include these:

- After surviving a bad motor vehicle accident that resulted in temporary cognitive impairment, my client utilized his time of healing to reevaluate his life and implement important changes.
- A client's overwhelming anxiety led her to join a meditation group. After a year of practice, she was able to get off her anxiety medication.

- A couple makes a bad financial decision that costs them a significant amount of money. As a result, they finally learn how to talk about finances in an effective way, allowing them to develop a plan for retirement savings, something they had been avoiding up to this point.
- A teenager goes through a painful break-up. He is depressed and withdrawn. His parents get him in to see a therapist and he begins to talk about issues of insecurity that have plagued him for years. He begins to blossom.

THE KITCHEN SINK

The truth is, there are literally hundreds of practices and techniques capable of supporting the process of change. You can think of the process of figuring out your particular combination of practices like a chef or a baker, tinkering with their recipes. You may add and subtract different ingredients until you get your recipe just right.

I have witnessed people make all manner of changes in all manner of ways. What matters most is what works for you. In my experience, change is less about using the right technique or the latest therapeutic trend, and more about a tenacious attitude on the part of the client combined with a solid therapeutic relationship.

Together, you and your therapist will be able to collaborate on the development of an effective treatment plan, complete with the skills necessary to work through whatever mental health challenges you face.

As I mentioned earlier in the chapter, the attitude that you bring to the endeavor of therapy is one of the most critical items within your control. Common sense tells us that different people approach novel experiences and the development of new habits differently. In her book *Better Than Before*, Gretchen Rubin identifies four distinct temperaments that she calls the Four Tendencies. These distinct types represent four characteristic ways people tend to approach change and habit formation. Developing a basic understanding of your tendency will help you crack the code on optimizing your personality, particularly in regard to overcoming procrastination, resistance to change, and other, similar obstacles to the establishment of new habits.

The truth is, it is normal to have some fear and resistance to the process of change. ***Inside each of us is both a desire for our lives to change and a desire to stay the same.*** As you begin your journey, honor the part of you that fears the unknown, but feed the part that is hungry for change and growth.

Chapter Ten

Beyond Personality—Exploring the Psyche

Developing a basic understanding of your psyche is an important step in addressing your psychological concerns. In ancient Greece, the word *psyche* referred to the soul; it was later defined as an "animating spirit" in sixteenth-century Latin. Today, the term *psyche* is associated with the mind.

Carl Jung, the visionary Swiss psychiatrist, described the psyche as "the totality of all psychic processes, conscious as well as unconscious." Jung viewed the psyche as a self-regulating, growth-oriented system that constantly seeks to balance opposing energies. Moving forward, I will be using Jung's definition. In order to deepen your understanding, let's break it down even further.

THE PSYCHE DEFINED

The psyche, while structurally complex, is both organized and purposeful. To put it another way, your psyche is an active, intelligent system that is both resource-rich and biased toward the fulfillment of your potential. Just as your physical body contains instructions to support natural development and mechanisms to fight off illness, your psychic structures are also growth-oriented and equipped with a psychological immune system.

For example, just as your body produces physical symptoms when there is an infection or disease process at work, your psyche also produces psychological symptoms when your emotional life is out of balance and changes are required.

With this framework in mind, you can learn to view psychological symptoms and personal crises—panic attacks, depressive episodes, unwanted obsessions, relationship meltdowns, recurrent accidents, existential angst—as the psyche's attempt to stimulate change. While it's easy to write off your problems as the result of a chemical imbalance or bad luck, they will continue to pursue you until the demands of the unconscious are met.

ANATOMY OF THE PSYCHE IN THREE PARTS

Imagine your psyche as a whole, made up of three parts: your personality, your unconscious mind, and your true Self. It may help to visualize the psyche as the three layers of the earth: crust, mantle, and core. The crust represents the personality, the part that is visible to both ourselves and others. The mantle represents the next layer down, the realm of the unconscious mind; while it exists below the surface, what goes on underground has a profound impact on the world above. And finally, the core represents the true Self, the essence of your being, the center from which everything flows.

PERSONALITY

Your personality is the most familiar, conscious manifestation of the psyche. Most people have a sense of their personality—enduring attitudes, thought patterns, behaviors, and preferences that are consistent over time. Perhaps you have taken a personality test such as the Myers-Briggs Type Indicator (MBTI), the Big Five, or the Enneagram. Understanding the fundamentals of your personality (and the personalities of those close to you) can benefit you tremendously.

From career and relationships to conflict style, learning to optimize the strengths of your personality while also making peace with its limitations can make daily life both easier and more satisfying. If you have not taken a personality inventory, I recommend starting with the free inventory offered by 16personalities.com. This empirically validated personality test is a combination of the Myers-Briggs Type Indicator and the Big Five personality traits. The website is also filled with useful articles and personal analytics to help you better understand your personality.

Another key component of your personality is your ego. And while the ego often gets a bad rap, it is a necessary part of the psyche. The role of the ego—including its pitfalls—is covered in the next chapter.

UNCONSCIOUS

Resting below the personality is the second layer of the psyche, the realm of the unconscious mind. Psychologists have hotly debated the nature of the unconscious for decades. Freud and Jung's epic relationship ended in part due to a fundamental disagreement about the nature of the unconscious. Freud believed that it was primarily made up of repressed sexual and aggressive drives, while Jung felt that the psyche was far more complex and nuanced. Jung believed there was a drive toward spiritual growth alive within the unconscious. He also proposed the existence of the collective unconscious, a dimension of shared, ancestral memories not borne of one's individual experiences.

Freud and Jung's debate was not the last one on the nature of the unconscious; psychologists, philosophers, and metaphysical pundits continue to offer theories on the nature of the unconscious mind today.

Given that your unconscious cannot be seen with the naked eye, we are ultimately left with a combination of theory and imagination to make sense of this mysterious terrain that resides outside the boundaries of conscious experience. Thankfully, there are tools that can provide you access to what lies below the surface of your awareness. Chief among them are dream analysis, which is discussed in detail in chapter 17.

The journey of psychotherapy provides ample opportunities to shed light on our unconscious patterns and thought processes.

As a matter of fact, one of the core tasks of therapy is to become more aware of your thoughts, feelings, and motivations. As you become more conscious of various aspects of your inner life and your patterns of behavior, you are likely to feel more alive and to have more freedom of movement.

Your therapist will be able to help you work with your unconscious in a productive way, guiding you toward insights that free up psychic energy. Specific examples include identifying the origins of self-defeating patterns, learning to feel and express emotions that you have historically avoided, diagnosing self-critical thought patterns, and ultimately tapping into unfulfilled potential.

This process often involves identifying and working with complexes and subpersonalities. I know what you may be thinking— "I didn't sign up for psychology 101!" But stay with me. This will make sense.

A *complex* is a fancy word for a pocket of repressed emotional energy, typically organized around a person or a theme—such as a mother complex, father complex, rescuer complex, or victim complex. Identifying your complexes will allow you to gain control over these subterranean forces that can steer your emotions and alter your decision-making.

Subpersonalities, similar to complexes, are energetic structures within the psyche that are automatically activated by specific psychosocial stressors. While that all may sound complicated, subpersonalities themselves are rather simple to identify. Examples of subpersonalities include the harsh critic, the wounded child, the angry victim, the perfect child, the rebel, and so forth. These so-called subpersonalities are essentially patterns of thoughts, feelings, and behaviors that were formed at critical times in your life when you were hurt, threatened, or overwhelmed by life.

Some subpersonalities represent wounded parts, while others represent protective parts. Even the self-destructive elements of your personality are trying to play a part in helping you to survive and not feel overwhelmed by painful emotions.

Hopefully, this quick overview of the unconscious will serve as a starting point for further conversations with your therapist. While there is much more that can be said about the topic, you now have a general overview of the terrain as well as some new terminology to assist you on your journey.

SELF

At the center of your psyche resides your Self. This third layer is your essence, what mystics believe to be your true identity.

Your Self is your deepest source of wisdom, creativity, energy, and purpose. When you experience a state of relaxed awareness, free of commentary and judgment, you are experiencing your true Self. When you are in the zone, feeling the rapture of being completely absorbed in the experience of the moment, you are experiencing your true Self.

The majority of spiritual practices are designed to increase your access to the Self. Activities such as art, music, theater, athletics, and the healing arts can help you to more fully experience the true Self. Infants and young children are a pure expression of the Self in its undeveloped form. The concepts in this book are all designed to help you develop greater access to your true Self. Indeed, all psychological health and spiritual growth flows both from and toward the Self.

IMAGINING YOUR PSYCHE

Given that the psyche is invisible, we are left with the language of metaphor to describe our inner lives. We have already explored the image of the psyche as the three layers of the earth. You can also think of your psyche as a house with many rooms. Some rooms are familiar—well furnished, decorated, and fully lived in—while other rooms remain a mystery, their contents hidden behind a locked door, waiting to be discovered. Or perhaps you prefer to view your psyche as a solar system, with each planet a different subpersonality, each one orbiting your radiant Self.

An image I find helpful for identifying and working with the subpersonalities of the unconscious is the metaphor of the inner committee. For most people, their psyche is dominated by one or two committee members (the usual suspects include the critic, the perfectionist, and the rebel). These dominant committee members force their will on the rest of the group. The question that begs to be asked is who else sits on the committee? What are the demands of the silent majority?

However you choose to view your psyche, it is important to become familiar with its different parts and how they relate to one another. Through a process of observation and inquiry, you can arrive at greater harmony within.

JOURNEY TOWARD WHOLENESS

Wholeness is the result of the psyche's movement toward balance and growth. When this process is supported and allowed to flourish, you can expect to experience a higher level of energy. You are likely to notice greater feelings of well-being and to see your projects come to fruition. In practical terms, this process of growth involves the trinity of self-discovery, self-acceptance, and self-expression.

Self-discovery requires your own personal combination of contemplative practices. *Self-acceptance* involves a thorough inventory of your strengths and weaknesses, allowing you to embrace your talents and accept your limitations. And finally, *self-expression* is the culmination of this process, allowing you to share your brilliance with the world. We will explore each of these ideas in greater depth in upcoming chapters. Together, these practices allow you to reach your full potential.

The journey toward wholeness provides tremendous emotional and energetic rewards. And while this process unfolds naturally across a lifetime, it can be accelerated by your efforts and with the help of psychotherapy. The ideas and exercises presented throughout this book are designed to support your psyche's natural journey toward growth and wholeness.

REAL-LIFE EXAMPLES

The psyche constantly seeks balance. Here are some examples of people moving toward balance in their lives:

—**Brian.** Overscheduled and in a hurry, Brian the extrovert decides to respond to the feelings of restlessness and discomfort that tug at him daily. He buys a journal and begins to write about his thoughts and feelings, as well as the whims of his imagination. As a result of his journaling, Brian becomes inspired to write a novel, something he has wanted to do for many years. While still an extrovert with a busy life, Brian now makes time for solitude and writing, thus cultivating his inner life and fulfilling his need for a creative outlet. As a result, he feels calm, content, and more complete.

—**Cherice.** An ambitious intellectual, Cherice is caught up in the world of thoughts and ideas. While she is successful in her career and socially adroit, she is woefully out of touch with her emotional life. This imbalance has led to a painful string of relationship mishaps. Motivated by the pain of her most recent break-up, she begins a course of therapy. Through conversations with her therapist, examination of her recurring dreams, and a deeper commitment to her yoga practice, she begins to develop greater emotional intelligence. This growing relationship with her emotional life, combined with more awareness of her body, allows Cherice to be more relaxed and present. She remains career-driven and intellectual, but now has greater self-awareness. As a result, she enjoys more satisfying intimate relationships.

—**Darren.** Known to all his friends as a nice guy, Darren joins a soccer team and begins to get in touch with his competitiveness and aggressive energy. His growth as a soccer player coincides with a greater ability to stand up for himself interpersonally. Speaking up about his wants and feelings with his fiancée and his friends has given Darren a greater sense of confidence and a higher level of energy. While still a peace-maker at heart, Darren now has a sense of his warrior spirit and his personal power. As a result, he is no longer depressed and chronically tired.

—**Mackenzie.** An introvert who loves books, cats, and quiet coffee shops, Mackenzie develops the courage to broaden her social circle through group hikes and weekly D&D campaigns. Her social anxiety begins to fade as she becomes more comfortable interacting with a broader range of people. Still an introvert and a homebody, she now has a growing community of support and connection. As a result, Mackenzie feels more confident and more connected to both others and herself.

As you can see with these examples, each person's journey involves both a respect for their inherent nature and a growth mentality. We must understand and accept who we are while also allowing for the changes required to be in balance.

ASK YOUR THERAPIST

Ask your therapist to help you—

- Identify your complexes and subpersonalities.
- Identify images and metaphors that allow you to visualize your psyche.
- Find ways to pursue self-discovery, self-acceptance, and self-expression.

Chapter Eleven

Ego, Self-Deception, and the Courage to Change

HUMAN BEINGS HAVE a remarkable capacity for self-deception. It's a funny thing, really—as a society, we value honesty at all costs, and yet, so often we lie to ourselves. The truth is, we each rely on a personal collection of persuasive story lines and tenacious defense mechanisms in order to maintain a sense of emotional equilibrium. This ongoing dance of self-deception, this chronic habit of avoidance, is done in the service of the ego.

Among other motivations (many of which are quite beneficial), the ego has a strong drive to defend against painful emotions and inconvenient truths. To put it simply, your ego likes to be comfortable, and it likes to be in control. If, however, you desire to lead an examined life, learning to overcome self-deception is critical. This chapter will help you identify and neutralize the many tricks of the ego.

EGO

In order to make sense of your proclivity for self-deception, you will need to first understand a few things about the nature of the ego.

Your ego is an essential part of your personality; without it, you would be unable to function in society. You can think of your ego as the command center of your executive functions—perception, judgment, planning, decision-making, reality testing, and other crucial cognitive tasks.

Picture your ego as the conductor of the orchestra, directing a myriad of mental activities. It is also a master of neutralizing emotional threats, prioritizing the maintenance of psychological security over all else. In this way, your ego is to your psyche what your immune system is to your body. And just as your immune system can overreact, causing serious health problems, your ego can also turn against you, causing serious problems within your psychological system.

DEFENSE MECHANISMS

Sigmund Freud identified and cataloged the primary defense mechanisms people utilize to protect themselves from disturbing emotions. And while we know that some of Freud's theories are antiquated and irrelevant, many of his discoveries were truly revolutionary.

Freud's theory of defense mechanisms was particularly brilliant. He gave us a useful vocabulary for describing the ego's tactics. A sampling of the most common defense mechanisms I see in my practice are **denial** (the attitude that a problem doesn't exist), **repression** (burying memories and emotions in the subconscious), **rationalizing** (justifying problematic attitudes and behavior through faulty reasoning), **minimizing** (downplaying the scope of a problem or behavior), and **projection** (assigning disowned traits of the Self onto others).

We all use some combination of these and other defense mechanisms to manage uncomfortable emotions. Which ones we favor is a function of our personality structure and the influence of our families.

Your therapist should be able to point out when you are using defense mechanisms to avoid your feelings or to justify problematic behaviors. Effective therapy designed to produce long-lasting results will require the exploration of these tactics of the ego. The reality is that we live with our emotions all of the time. The question is, are they steering you at an unconscious level? Or are you consciously expressing them?

SELF-DECEPTION IN RELATIONSHIPS

As Flannery O'Connor once said, "The truth does not change according to our ability to stomach it." And yet, how do you get through to powerful people with strong defense mechanisms? Truth telling can be very powerful indeed. But sometimes we need a new framework, complete with new language, in order to penetrate the deeply rooted habits of self-deception.

The book *Leadership and Self-Deception,* written by the Arbinger Institute for business executives—but with plenty of wisdom for everyone else—presents several compelling examples of what self-deception looks like on the interpersonal level, especially in the workplace. In each case, self-deception is the direct result of a betrayal of one's core values.

For example, imagine the following scenario. Your newborn infant wakes up crying for the umpteenth time in one night. You know it's your turn to get out of bed and check on the baby, but you don't, waiting instead for your partner to tend to the baby. In order to neutralize the guilt you feel for letting your partner down, you tell yourself a story about how your partner is the selfish one.

Other common examples of this kind of self-deception include the use of narratives about why your coworkers are so difficult and incompetent, or how homeless people made bad choices to end up where they are. And while there may be some truth to your ideas, the real motivation for your story lines is to create emotional distance and manage cognitive dissonance. These unconscious exercises of self-deception are the ego's attempts to be free of the pressure to respond to feelings of concern for a fellow human being, and to avoid the challenge of dealing with difficult, interpersonal issues head-on.

The authors describe this kind of distorted thinking as "being in the box." From inside the box, one begins to view other people as objects who are in the way, not as subjects with their own interests. We all fall prey to this mindset from time to time, and it provides the justification for treating others poorly. This mental process happens rapidly, often just below the surface of awareness. But once one becomes aware of this tendency toward self-deception, and also commits to placing values into action, real change can occur.

THE COURAGE TO BE A DIFFERENT PERSON

People resist change for lots of different reasons. Chief among them is our attachment to our identity. Even if you know certain changes are good for you, there may be a part of you that is afraid of letting go of the person you know so well, even the parts that cause you unnecessary suffering.

Change requires a leap of faith. There is a point at which you let go of an old part of your identity before the new version of you is fully formed, and that interim space can feel strange and uncomfortable. But over time, you will grow into your new Self. Just as a snake sheds its skin as it grows, we too outgrow older versions of ourselves.

Adam Horovitz of the Beastie Boys was once called out as a hypocrite for the lyrics he wrote on "Song for the Man." The song is a stark contrast from the unconscious, misogynistic lyrical content of their early years. It challenges the way men often objectify women. In response to the challenge, Horovitz replied: "I would rather be a hypocrite than the same person for the rest of my life."

If your therapeutic goals involve significant changes to your behavior and changes to who you are in the world, you may need to overcome the fear of how others will judge your path. More times than I can count, a client has made the argument that attempting certain changes feels insincere, as if they are being a fraud. It's true that trying out new behaviors and new ways of thinking can feel strange and unfamiliar at first. Like a new pair of shoes or a radically different haircut, it takes time to adjust to a new version of yourself. Just remember, the part of you that is resistant to change is your ego, not your true Self.

PUTTING IT INTO PRACTICE

Why even bother? Overcoming self-deception is hard, painful work. Perhaps that is why most people either don't try to become truly honest with themselves at all, or only go so far with the endeavor. And yet, there are those intrepid adventurers among us, driven by insatiable curiosity and the determination to reach their full potential, who decide to pursue this difficult goal.

When doing something hard, it is important to remember your "why." Why do you want to master the cello, get a PhD, run a marathon, climb a 14,000-foot mountain, learn to speak Italian, join the Peace Corps, or attempt any other difficult pursuit? When you remember your why, it's easier to keep going. Self-deception, by its very nature, is elusive. You will need a combination of curiosity, courage, commitment, and self-compassion to overcome this challenge. And you will have to repeat this process over and over.

Let's face it, it's not easy to digest critical feedback. It's painful to face our own failings, to see our mistakes, to reckon with our limitations. But if real change is what you are after, then this is a crucial step along the way. Most people like the idea of change. And yet, when faced with the hard work of addressing undesirable, shadow qualities, many choose to maintain the status quo. If you are truly committed to this practice, ask for feedback from people in your life whom you trust. And then be prepared to face the music. It may knock the wind out of you. But once you recover, you will be stronger and more self-aware.

Chapter Twelve

Happiness Reconsidered

The desire to be happy is universal. The problem is, you can easily get confused about what truly makes a person happy. To make matters worse, the quest for happiness may interfere with natural opportunities to experience joy. In this chapter, I will challenge conventional wisdom on the pursuit of happiness and explore an alternate, more reliable approach to feeling good, grounded in the principle of energy.

A MISGUIDED QUEST

In his groundbreaking and refreshingly irreverent book, *The Subtle Art of Not Giving a F*ck*, Mark Manson makes the salient point that the quest to obtain something implies that you do not have it. As a result, the search for happiness paradoxically takes you in the opposite direction from your intended destination. Manson's diagnosis hits the nail on the head, Our culture's collective obsession with the pursuit of happiness isn't going so well. If we were on the right track, rates of depression and other mental illnesses would be going down, not surging upward, year after year.

The way I see it, the feeling of happiness cannot be bought or captured. The more compulsively you pursue happiness, the more elusive it becomes, like a beautiful butterfly that always escapes your net.

Harvard social psychologist and author Daniel Gilbert makes a similar set of observations in his groundbreaking book, *Stumbling on Happiness*. Drawing upon dozens of studies, Gilbert points out that human beings, while unique among other animals in our ability to anticipate the future, are generally pretty bad at predicting how we will feel when the future arrives. Our failure of prognostication is particularly relevant to the issue of happiness. As we attempt to plan for our future, making decisions designed to maximize our pleasure and contentment, we look forward through the lens of our present experience. As a result, the way we feel *now* shapes our predictions regarding how we might feel *later*, rendering us unreliable when it comes to deciding what will make us happy and what will make us miserable.

To go a step further, being happy all of the time is not a realistic goal. Those who lay claim to a state of perpetual bliss deserve your skepticism; they are more than likely presenting you with a façade of happiness, not a joy that radiates from within. What then, you may be wondering, is the alternative to the pursuit of happiness?

The alternative is the principle of energy. Throughout the remainder of the chapter, we will explore how you can tap into ordinary daily experiences in order to maximize your energetic potential. In other words, when you pursue activities that make you feel alive, happiness often follows.

THE PRINCIPLE OF ENERGY

Early in my training, my mentor impressed upon me the importance of doing everything possible to raise my energy level to its full potential and to help my clients do the same. With great enthusiasm, he explained that the cultivation of stable energy is the prime objective. Underlying this principle is the notion that *the psyche is fundamentally energetic*. When you feel frustrated by low energy, you can be sure that the culprit is either biological in nature (not enough sleep, not eating well, illness, or other problems with the body) or psychological (the consequence of blocking the natural flow of psychic energy).

This formula has become a guiding principle in my clinical practice. It is also a mindset that I live by, as it consistently works. As a result, I am always on the lookout for the flow of energy. Where is it coming from? Where is it going? Why does it get stuck? Ultimately, the point is to get your ego out of the way, allowing your energy to have its natural movement. Making this principle a part of your toolkit will greatly benefit your journey toward psychological health.

Energy can be found everywhere. It's in a smile shared with a stranger, in a good laugh with friends, in a deep breath as you step outside to greet the day. Energy awaits in the expression of your creativity, in the discovery of novel insights, and in the expression of truth.

Energetic rewards are also abundant when you participate in the most vital aspects of life, such as deepening your relationships with loved ones, cultivating creative outlets, pursuing spiritual growth, and seeking ways to live according to your deepest values.

These are just a handful of examples of the kinds of experiences that have the potential to raise your energy. When you are psychologically healthy, you will naturally engage in activities that support the flow of energy. But when you are anxious or depressed, angry or obsessed, caught in the grip of addictions, or otherwise imbalanced, you are more vulnerable to either avoiding or blocking the natural flow of your psychic energy. One of the ways people block the flow of psychic energy is, ironically, in the quest for happiness. If your coordinates are off, you will end up on the wrong end of the map.

Returning to the principle of energy as an alternative to happiness, there is tremendous energy to be found in the honest expression of emotion. One of the surest ways to put this concept into practice is to learn to be aware of and express what you are feeling as consistently as possible.

Every emotion has energy. When you ignore or block your emotions, you lower your energy level; when you identify and express your emotions, you preserve your energy. When you are sad, cry. When you're afraid, acknowledge your fear. When something strikes you as funny, laugh. When you feel awe, express your wonderment. When you feel angry, seek a healthy outlet. When you feel the impulse to be creative, pursue your passion. When you feel joy, share it with others.

While the formula is simple, it requires tremendous dedication to implement. Living in this manner will ensure that your energy level is as high as possible. You won't be happy all of the time, but you will feel both genuine and alive.

GETTING INTO THE ZONE

Artists, actors, musicians, and athletes all know what it's like to be in the zone, Anyone who has a talent or passion that they get lost in has had a taste of this state of mind. The zone is a state of flowing energy where the mind becomes quiet, allowing things to happen naturally. You lose track of time, becoming lost in what you are doing. Your mind is at peace while your body moves with ease, performing at a high level. Creative ideas arise naturally. The experience of being in the zone is its own reward.

Hungarian-American psychologist Mihaly Csikszentmihalyi spent much of his career studying the zone, an experience he refers to as *flow*. Flow states are intrinsically rewarding, frequently causing the Self to become more complex as a response to greater and greater challenges. The emotional rewards that result from being in a flow state cannot be matched by external achievements.

The zone is not only the domain of accomplished athletes and skilled creatives. It is a state of being that is available to everyone. As a matter of fact, with practice, you can learn to move through the daily demands of professional responsibilities and domestic life while being in the zone. The key is to learn to harmonize your body and mind with your environment. Living in this way supports a higher energetic state, one likely to yield feelings of well-being.

YOUR NATURAL STATE

Close your eyes and imagine how you feel on your best day. Pay attention to how your body feels, to your mental and emotional state, and to anything else that you are aware of. This is your natural state, your energetic potential. You can think of this state of awareness as another way to get in the zone.

Remembering our discussion of the anatomy of the psyche from chapter 10, your natural state, the zone, and your true Self are all one and the same. The goal is to spend as much time as possible in this higher, energetic state, centered in the Self. Using the concepts and practices discussed throughout this book, you can develop the ability to spend more and more time in your natural state.

Here is a homework assignment I often give to my clients. Be on the lookout for the next time that you feel fully alive and at your mental and emotional best. For some of you, this will be a regular occurrence; for others, this state may be fleeting and rare. Once you are there, take notice of everything that you are aware of. Notice how your body feels, the rhythm of your breathing, your state of mind, the content of your thoughts, your emotional state, and anything else that seems relevant or interesting.

Once you have thoroughly observed your experience, see how long you can sustain it. It could be for a minute, for an hour, for a day, or longer. As soon as anything—internal or external—disrupts this state, make a note of what it was that caused the change. Repeat this process. This exercise has the following objectives:

- Extending the amount of time that you spend in your natural state
- Identifying obstacles to residing in the natural state of true self-expression
- Establishing a balanced, energetic state as your new baseline state of being

---

ASK YOUR THERAPIST

Ask your therapist to help you identify any obstacles to expressing your fully alive, energetic Self. Assuming that you are well rested and physically healthy, blockages typically fall into two categories: (1) blocked self-expression, and (2) unfulfilled purpose. Examples of blocked self-expression include being unable to grieve, cry, express anger, stand up for yourself, think critically, enjoy being sexual, have original opinions, and be decisive. Examples of unfulfilled purpose include lack of creative outlets, not living according to one's values, ignoring one's spirituality, forsaking important personal ambitions, and doing work that is incompatible with your talents and core values. Exploring these areas with your therapist can yield tremendous results—both in the area of symptom relief and overall life satisfaction.

Learning how to calibrate your energy level offers tremendous advantages in life. Whatever your therapy goals may be, developing the ability to actively raise your energy level will greatly benefit you, and happiness may just follow.

We have determined that the quest for happiness, while a universal impulse, can more often than not become problematic. Rather than seeking to be happy, it is better to seek aliveness and authenticity. This can be achieved through embracing each emotion, recognizing the energetic power of honest expression. The feeling of fulfillment and aliveness can also be increased by living according to one's values, with a deeper sense of purpose and meaning. The next chapter will take you further on the path of exploring these perennial questions of values, purpose, and meaning.

Chapter Thirteen

The Big Picture: Values, Purpose, and Meaning

Values, purpose, and meaning do not belong solely to the domain of philosophers, theologians, and mystics. Psychotherapy must also concern itself with these crucial questions.

As we have established, living in harmony with your core values leads to greater energy and well-being. Furthermore, having a clear sense of purpose can significantly increase your sense of fulfillment in life. Though intangible, these elements of your psyche are vital, possessing the power to both shape your identity and govern your decisions. More importantly, if you resist or ignore these critical aspects of yourself, you are sure to suffer the consequences of emotional malaise. Bringing these key elements of your identity into focus is the purpose of this chapter.

My goal is to help you solidify these aspects of yourself and assist you in translating your values and purpose into action. While we are on this leg of our journey, we will also take a look at how the creation of meaning can provide tremendous solace amid the suffering and hardship that life can dish out.

VALUES

Who are your greatest inspirations in life? Chances are, the people you most admire have a deep set of values that they live by. From my point of view, values represent the intersection of passion, conviction, and identity. Values are an expression of your ethical code, your moral compass. Additionally, values can play a key role in your efforts to be an authentic person in your dealings with others. Knowing where you stand and what is important to you is critical to living a fulfilling life in a world filled with a never-ending barrage of distractions and propaganda.

Cassius Clay changed his name to Muhammad Ali and later refused to serve in the US Army on the basis of his moral values and religious beliefs. He did all of this in spite of public criticism and a three-and-a-half-year interruption to his boxing career. Temple Grandin pursued a career in animal science due to her passion for the welfare of animals, in spite of her autism and in the face of tremendous resistance from a heavily male-dominated profession. Grandin and Ali represent two individuals with deeply held values that were translated into action for the benefit of the world.

As you begin to think about your own values, consider asking yourself some questions. Who are your role models? What stirs your soul? What are you willing to work hard and make sacrifices for? What truly matters to you at the deepest level? These and other similar questions can guide you toward the discovery (or rediscovery) of your core values.

Given the importance of the topic, how do you go about determining your values? You can start by taking a close look at how you spend your time and your money. As the old saying goes, actions speak louder than words. We all know workaholics who claim that family is their number one priority and we have all seen examples of religious zealots whose personal lives are engulfed in scandal. But before you begin making any value judgments, please read on. The truth is we all contain a multitude of contradictions, hypocrisies, and moral inconsistencies. And no one is immune to self-deception. In my case, preserving the environment is one of my core values—yet I love to eat meat, which has a large carbon footprint. Knowing this, I make a concerted effort to limit my meat consumption and, whenever possible, to get my meat from free-range farms.

The point is to start where you are. Make an honest and thorough inventory of how you are living your life today. One of the best ways to proceed is to engage in some form of contemplative practice. Such activities include journaling, meditation, or simply taking a walk in the woods, allowing your mind to wander. There are also plenty of helpful exercises available to help you get in touch with your values. Brené Brown offers a fantastic list of possible core values in her book, *Dare to Lead*, along with guidance for narrowing down your own values.

You can also talk with your therapist about your quest to identify your core values. However you go about it, it is important to make a commitment to this process. Investing time fine-tuning your value system can be rewarding; it has the potential to bring vigor and focus to your endeavors.

The topic of values is not complete without discussing priorities. In my view, knowing your values and making a genuine attempt to live by them will allow you to naturally prioritize well. Values are enduring; priorities change from day to day. If you are rooted in your core values, you will be able to choose among competing priorities.

PURPOSE

Living with purpose can lead to a life of passion and vitality, ultimately yielding a greater sense of overall satisfaction. When you know your purpose, you will find you are motivated to overcome obstacles, to persevere in the face of challenges, as you are driven by this inner flame. A purposeful life requires that you live for more than pleasure and comfort. For some, purpose manifests itself as a calling to a particular career or life path, while for others it can be more abstract. No matter what your purpose is, you will feel it in your bones when it becomes known to you. Here are some examples of the forms that purpose can take:

- Service
- Leadership

- Vocation
- Creative expression
- Spirituality
- Activism
- Parenting
- Community building

These are just a handful of examples of how others have discovered purpose in life. Moving through life without a clear sense of purpose can lead to feelings of emptiness and despair. The same contemplative practices just listed for clarifying your values can also assist you in clarifying your purpose.

If your quest to discover your purpose has not yielded results, do not despair. As someone who is a lifelong seeker of truth, I have found that the journey is more important than the destination. The way that I see it, there are some lucky souls who know who they are and what they want from a young age. They surge forward in life like a blazing arrow trained at their target. And then there are those of us whose path is more of a long and winding road, full of switchbacks, detours, and the occasional dead end. If your purpose in life isn't making itself known in spite of your searching, keep your chin up. The journey of self-discovery contains tremendous value and meaning.

MEANING

Whether agnostic, atheist, spiritual, or religious, everyone seeks to make sense out of the world around them. Throughout history, shamans, priests, and rabbis offered wisdom and guidance. These teachings from spiritual elders helped humankind to feel connected to each other and to live in harmony with the great mysteries of the world. Moreover, for most of human history, making sense of life's perennial questions was not a priority, as most people were preoccupied with the toil of daily life.

Deeply entrenched cultural attitudes and social hierarchies have historically been powerful enough to discourage the average person from asking tough questions such as What is the meaning of life? and Why do bad things happen to good people? But times have changed.

For many people, organized religion provides a deep sense of purpose, identity, and moral guidance, grounded in a community with a shared belief system. But for many others, the road less traveled beckons, offering a much-needed alternative to traditional religious pathways.

Embarking upon your own path can lead to positive feelings of liberation and freedom. But the quest to find your own way can also become a burden. Attempting to make sense of a chaotic world all on your own can easily feel overwhelming. The weight of these existential questions leads many to a state of cynicism, apathy, and dread.

But do not despair. There is a third way, grounded in neither religious dogma nor cynical apathy. This path involves the creation of meaning through a commitment to something greater than yourself. Make no mistake—this is not a cakewalk. It requires a deep level of commitment as well as dedication to practice.

In Viktor Frankl's classic book, *Man's Search for Meaning*, he recounts his harrowing experiences as a prisoner of Nazi concentration camps during World War II. Frankl noted that in spite of the dire circumstances and tremendous suffering, many of the prisoners were able to find meaning within their situation. Those who were able to connect to a sense of hope, meaning, or spirituality fared much better than those prisoners who gave in to feelings of despair.

In the modern era, the feeling of despair is sadly not in short supply. Pick a problem—the COVID-19 pandemic, climate change, income inequality, institutional racism, population explosion, political corruption, the polarization of society, the rise of violent extremism, the overwhelming din of social media, and the list goes on. And yet, human beings continue to adapt and endure, finding innovative ways to transform overwhelming circumstances, becoming more advanced along the way. Given all this, the question that remains is this: How do we create meaning out of the circumstances we are given?

FINDING YOUR PATH

While it's not my place to suggest which path is right for you, I do strongly believe that it helps to have a positive path to follow. It could be

- A commitment to service,
- A personal source of meaning,
- Devotion to a particular religion,
- A personal relationship to a higher power,
- A spiritual practice, or
- A deep reverence for the natural world.

The important thing is to connect to something larger than yourself, to put your faith in something that encourages a meaningful way to exist in the world.

In *Cutting Through Spiritual Materialism*, Tibetan Buddhist teacher Chögyam Trungpa makes the astute observation that many Westerners engage in a dangerous habit that he calls "spiritual materialism." This subtle form of self-deception involves the collecting of spiritual teachings, the amassing of enlightened ideas and New Age concepts. While the appearance of the endeavor is one of spiritual growth and deepening maturity, the ego has cleverly become the driver of the project. In other words, it's easy to become identified with spiritual concepts that make you feel good, as you jump from one path to another.

Genuine spiritual growth develops slowly, as a result of choosing a path and sticking to it. Day after day, year after year, you follow the path, even when the going gets tough. Neither the development of meaning, nor the path of spiritual growth are flashy or exciting. With a commitment to the journey, you are sure to reap great rewards.

In my clinical experience, people with a strong connection to faith, spirituality, or a cause greater than themselves are both more resilient and more fulfilled. Unfortunately, some therapists shy away from discussing matters of faith and meaning, which is sadly a lost opportunity. If these areas are important to you, let your therapist know. If the topic of spirituality and meaning is foreign, consider adding it to your list of topics for consideration.

This chapter represents a brief introduction to the concepts of values, purpose, and meaning. Exploring these ideas in greater depth can be a lifelong endeavor. Taking time to investigate these questions with your counselor can add an important dimension to your journey of therapy. While having deeply rooted values or a well-developed spiritual life cannot remove the suffering of life, it can make the suffering more bearable.

Chapter Fourteen

The Hero's Journey

WHAT STORY ARE you living in? Are you the hero or are you a victim? Are you the author of your life or a passive character in someone else's tale?

The answer to these questions can reveal much about your attitude toward life. Human beings are storytellers, and the stories that we tell have great power, determining how we feel about our lives while defining the limits of our imagination. Thankfully, we each have the power to alter and change our stories. Ultimately, learning to see yourself as a hero on a journey is an important step toward personal empowerment.

In this chapter, we will unpack the meaning of the hero archetype, as we explore how this concept relates to your psychotherapy journey. It's no accident that epic stories such as *Star Wars*, *The Lord of the Rings*, *Harry Potter*, Marvel Cinematic Universe, and countless others are so successful and beloved. The reason for their appeal goes beyond the way they entertain us. These tales speak to us on a soul level. The narrative structure touches something deep within, awakening a universal longing for exploration, adventure, and transformation.

YOU ARE THE HERO

The stories listed above are all examples of the hero's journey, an ancient blueprint found cross-culturally and told in many forms. In the past century, psychologists and mythologists such as Carl Jung, Joseph Campbell, and others have analyzed and amplified the psychological significance of these universal tales of adventure and discovery. The problem to be solved is this—when you read or watch stories of heroic adventure without seeing yourself reflected in the hero, you are missing the point. *You are the hero.*

In other words, it's psychologically lazy to project your own strength, courage, and virtue onto others. Whether in fiction or real life, many of us put others on a pedestal while devaluing our own brilliance. Once you place yourself into the role of hero within your own story, only then can you gain access to the full power and energetic resources awaiting you in your unconscious.

STAGES OF THE JOURNEY

How, you might be asking, do such heroic tales relate to your experience of being in therapy? In the hero's journey, the hero goes through a series of familiar experiences— the call to adventure, refusal of the call, leaving home, meeting allies, facing trials, developing new abilities, overcoming adversity, personal transformation, and returning home. This sequence of events perfectly mirrors the process of transformation one undergoes when committed to personal growth and psychotherapy.

Your problems are the call to adventure. If you are like most people, you initially refused the call to change, putting off looking for a therapist. Leaving home represents letting go of your defenses and stepping outside of your comfort zone. Your therapist and your loved ones who help you along the way are your allies. Over time, life itself becomes your teacher. The trials of the hero's journey are the personal issues you must face, and in the process of working through them, you develop new skills and greater maturity. Ultimately, you return home to your Self, enjoying the benefits of your dedication and hard work. You are now ready to share your newfound wisdom with others.

When facing difficult circumstances, it can be helpful to place your personal story into a larger context. If you are able to see yourself as a hero on a journey, new perspectives and possibilities begin to arise. Approaching your situation in this way is the opposite of the so-called victim mentality. As Joseph Campbell once said, "The cave you fear to enter holds the treasure you seek."

The viewpoint of the hero's journey can help you feel more connected to others—even your ancestors—who have walked a similar path before you. When we are hurting and suffering, we so often feel alone. Seeing yourself as a hero on a journey reminds you of your connection to others, and to a larger story.

Whether you are struggling with depression, anxiety, addictions, obsessions, unresolved trauma, relationship problems, or grief, the concept of the hero's journey can apply to you. You are a hero and your journey is calling.

Chapter Fifteen

Insight and Action: How to Reach Your Full Potential

Insight and action work together like an architect and a builder, powering the engines of change. When harnessed together, insight and action can help you to realize your full potential, transforming your goals into reality. When they are not in sync, however, your results can be diminished. In this chapter of our journey, we will explore how to put these concepts into practice.

INSIGHT

Psychological insight can present itself as the classic aha moment, the proverbial light bulb illuminating a long-standing issue. Some insights are hard won, the result of intensive work; others arrive spontaneously, an unexpected gift from the subconscious. Either way, insights offer a shift of perspective that brings clarity to an issue. When you gain insight into the origin of a problem—unwanted feelings, self-defeating relationship patterns, a mental obsession, or a stubborn habit—the feeling of liberation can be tremendous. Such discoveries are almost guaranteed to free up emotional energy.

A positive therapy experience can significantly improve your chances of arriving at important insights about yourself. In order for this to occur, however, you and your therapist must work together. You will need to explore all possible angles of your situation. Your therapist will walk beside you, serving as your guide as you make your journey of change. Their training and experience provide the maps that will assist you in navigating this unfamiliar terrain.

In order for the journey toward insight to be successful, much will be required of you as well. Curiosity and emotional vulnerability are the tools that you will need to bring on this journey. Without an attitude of curiosity about yourself, little progress can be made. Furthermore, if you are unable to let your guard down, to become emotionally vulnerable and open, limited changes can occur. While such a journey can be emotionally trying, there is a promise of great rewards.

ACTION

While insights are liberating, they are seldom enough to help you reach your goals. A therapy experience that's full of insight but lacking a plan for action can get lost in the clouds. To put it another way, *seeing something differently is illuminating; doing something differently is empowering.* When you begin to try out new behaviors and experiment with new, authentic forms of self-expression, you allow your true Self to be expressed.

For some, taking action can be more challenging than arriving at novel insights. New behaviors often involve stepping outside of your comfort zone, in some cases crossing an invisible foul line. For example, expressing yourself in new ways (boundary setting, speaking your mind, being vulnerable, taking risks) can cause you to experience anxiety. If this is the case, your anxiety is most likely due to blocked emotional energy, or conditioned guilt associated with things you were forbidden from doing during sensitive, developmental years. These remnants of childhood conditioning can be strong enough to discourage you from taking action, thus obstructing your path toward the realization of your full potential. Given all this, it is extremely important to fight past the pitfalls of conditioned guilt and anxiety.

To put it another way, your curiosity about new experiences must be greater than your fear of change. The tools necessary for this stage of the journey are courage and commitment. Along with curiosity and openheartedness, you will need to draw upon your courage to persevere in the face of difficult emotions. A firm commitment to a plan of action will provide the determination to stay the course.

With each victory, your confidence in your ability to take meaningful action will be sure to grow. As irrational feelings become more manageable, new, positive behaviors and habits can take root.

Following are some examples of individuals who put insights into action.

REAL-LIFE EXAMPLES

—**Javier**. After months in therapy, Javier develops insight into his tendency to avoid conflict. This habit stems from his efforts to keep the peace in his volatile family when he was a child. Understanding that he is now a fully capable adult with greater physical, mental, and financial resources, he begins to stand up for himself. Even though such confrontations raise his anxiety, Javier begins to see positive results from his efforts. These victories lead to a greater sense of confidence and self-worth. As a result, Javier now enjoys more frequent promotions at work and stronger emotional connections at home.

—**Beth**. Beth discovers a pattern of yelling at her spouse and children when she feels overwhelmed, much like her parents yelled at her many years ago. Beth follows up on her discovery with a firm commitment to stop taking out her stress on her loved ones. Having made a commitment, Beth also makes a plan of action: (1) working on her anger becomes her top priority in therapy; (2) she reads books on anger management; (3) she rehearses ways to appropriately express anger; and (4) she practices regular self-care. While still experiencing intense anger from time to time, Beth is now free from feelings of shame and self-loathing that would historically follow her angry tirades. Consequently, Beth's relationships with family members have improved dramatically.

—**Michael**. Michael becomes honest with himself about his addiction to social media and online activity. He has the insight that this compulsive behavior is driven by his insecurities. Having accepted the truth of his situation, Michael begins to identify his core values and to courageously pursue his dreams. He translates this insight into action with a commitment to limit his time online, thus freeing up vast opportunities for both personal and professional growth.

As you begin your journey of therapy, it is important to be patient with the process and to be prepared to take the insights won in the therapy office out into the world.

Chapter Sixteen

Nature: The Healing Power of the Great Outdoors

If I ask you to close your eyes and picture yourself in the most relaxing and peaceful place you can imagine, chances are you will choose somewhere in nature. This place is where you would go if you could be anywhere in the world, a place where you are sure to feel at home and at peace. Perhaps you picture yourself hiking in a pristine aspen grove high up in the Rocky Mountains. Maybe you are sinking your toes into the sand on a beautiful Pacific beach. Or perhaps you see yourself gazing out the window of a cozy log cabin nestled in the rolling hills of the Ozarks.

Going beyond vacation getaways, think of the times you have taken a walk to clear your head and get some fresh air. We all have the desire to get away, to retreat, to get a break from the overwhelming stress of life. Nature is where we so often turn when we are looking for that combination of comfort, healing, and escape.

NATURE IS AWESOME

As John Muir once remarked, "In every walk with nature one receives far more than he seeks." Of all the things that bring us to a state of rapture and wonderment—the birth of a child, a sublime piece of music, an artistic masterpiece, a profound expression of kindness—nature has to be one of the most reliable at producing feelings of awe.

Perhaps for you it was the first time you saw the ocean, a summer vacation at the Grand Canyon, or a hike through snow-capped mountains. Wherever those formative experiences occurred—now tattooed in your memory forever—they have made an energetic imprint that will stay with you throughout your lifetime. Nature can also touch you in profound ways, right where you are. Perhaps you feel a sense of awe taking in the sunset from your front porch, watching birds gather at the feeder outside your kitchen window, or looking closely at the delicate colors of wildflowers along the side of the road. The beauty and wonder of nature is all around us, and it has the power to both inspire and heal.

I have a vivid memory of walking in the redwoods of Northern California when I decided, once and for all, to be a therapist. Having wrestled with the question off and on for a year following my graduation from college, clarity came to me in the forest. The combination of my conversation with my friend and the stunning beauty of the surrounding nature—towering redwoods, magnificent ferns, and a peaceful stillness unrivaled anywhere I have been—allowed me to arrive at my truth. And while it was transformative, I know in my gut that this is no unusual story.

Without a doubt, most people have a story of a profound experience in nature. I have a friend whose battle with suicidal feelings dissolved after a reflective experience at the ocean. Many of my clients regularly seek refuge and restoration in nature.

The therapeutic value of nature cannot be overstated. Spending time outside, allowing your senses to bathe in the sights, sounds, smells, and textures of the natural world is inherently restorative and healing. It's that simple. And a growing body of research offers empirical support for this simple truth, something most of us have intuitively known our whole lives.

EMPIRICAL EVIDENCE ON THE POWER OF NATURE

In her book *The Nature Fix*, Florence Williams takes the reader around the world as she stitches together compelling stories and promising research findings on the many ways nature makes us "healthier, happier, and more creative." After a jarring move from Boulder, Colorado, to Washington, DC, Williams was motivated to explore how our connection with nature influences both health and cognition, digging deeply into exactly what more time in nature has in store for us.

Williams visits both Korea and Japan, where the practice of "forest bathing" is being studied. It turns out that a leisurely walk in the forest lowers cortisol—your body's primary stress hormone—significantly more than an urban stroll of equal time. That same nature walk will also lead to a decrease in negative ruminations, studies show.

The author enjoys a trip to the Utah desert with a crew of intrepid neuroscientists who share a collective interest in the study of attention. It appears that nature may hold the answer to many of the problems of distress and distractibility that result from living in an ever-plugged-in world.

It turns out that exposure to nature can actually foster healing. Perhaps you are familiar with Roger Ulrich's famous hospital window study (published in *Science*, 1984) that demonstrated surgical patients with green views from their hospital room recovered faster and required less pain medication than their counterparts without a view of nature. Their nurses also noted that the patients with a view of nature had a better attitude.

From five hours per month in nature (the minimum point at which you begin to significantly notice increased feelings of well-being) to the "three-day effect" (the phenomenon in which longer periods of time in nature, sans technology, begin to change us in deeper ways), the positive impact of nature is now being verified by science.

REMEMBERING OUR ORIGINAL CONNECTION

The human mind loves to organize, sort, and label. We are quick to separate the world into binary categories, especially where the natural world and the man-made environment are concerned. And while these are logical divisions—town versus country, organic versus synthetic—we often forget that *we are a part of nature.* Everything humans have invented and fabricated originally came from natural resources found within the earth.

This connection is easy to forget, as we spend most of our time in climate-controlled, artificially lit, indoor environments. So how do we begin to break down these categories and remember our fundamental connection to the natural world?

BRINGING NATURE HOME

The most obvious way to tap into the healing benefits of nature is to spend more time in the wilderness. Activities such as hiking, camping, fishing, hunting, canoeing, backpacking, and mountain biking are all fantastic ways to enjoy the great outdoors. And yet, there are many other great ways to connect with nature that don't require a garage full of recreational gear and a long drive out to the country.

For many people who live in large cities, getting out of town to get lost in nature is more of a special treat than a regular part of the daily routine. We must, therefore, find ways to wake up to the natural elements around us, to enjoy slices of nature within the urban environment. Here are some simple ideas to enhance your connection to nature:

- Take a daily walk in your neighborhood.
- Visit a nearby park.
- Read a book on your porch or balcony.
- Add house plants to your home or office.
- Start a garden.
- Get a bird feeder.

- Get a pet.
- Get involved with a local environmental organization.

FEEDING YOUR SOUL

The way I see it, cultivating a deeper relationship with nature is both good for the body and good for the soul. While we each require a unique recipe of ingredients to thrive, we share a common humanity through our connection to our ancestors.

For 99 percent of human history, people lived on the land, completely dependent on the natural world for survival and recreation. Our daily rhythms were shaped by the changing seasons and the availability of food. It's only in recent history that we have benefited from electricity, factory farming, mass transportation, modern medicine, and other such advances. And while these technologies have clearly extended our lifespans and expanded our comfort, there have been some big losses along the way. I believe that these rapid and dramatic changes are partly to blame for the epidemic of anxiety, depression, loneliness, and apathy that threaten our communities.

While nature alone cannot cure our emotional maladies, it is an essential ingredient in helping us to become whole again. So put down this book and go outside.

Chapter Seventeen

Dreams: The Forgotten Ally

Your dreams—those bizarre, ever-changing movies that occupy your mind night after night—hold the keys to emotional regulation, problem solving, and creative inspiration. Modern scientific discoveries are beginning to confirm what the sages of old have long known. Our dreams have much to teach us. In this chapter we will take a deep dive into the mysterious and fascinating world of dreams and dream analysis.

ANCIENT AND MODERN VIEWS ON DREAMS

Dreams have been revered cross-culturally for centuries. In ancient Egypt and ancient Greece, dreams were seen as messengers from the gods. As a matter of fact, nearly every religious tradition is steeped in myths involving prophetic dreams that foretell the coming of a savior or an anointed leader. Joseph was told of Mary's pregnancy in a dream; she was instructed to name the child Jesus. The Buddha's mother dreamed her bed was taken to a mountain peak where her side was painlessly pierced by the shining tusk of an elephant. She awoke knowing she had immaculately conceived. Much of the Koran was revealed to the prophet Muhammad through dreams.

To this day, many indigenous cultures regularly discuss and consult dreams as a community, carefully heeding their messages. And while modern psychology and neurology have located the origin of dreams in the brain, many mysteries still remain.

Contemporary research into the function of sleep and dreams continues to reveal new discoveries about the purpose of our nighttime narratives, including both cognitive and emotional benefits. From problem solving and memory consolidation to emotional catharsis, your dreams are the crown jewel of your unconscious mind. If you follow the advice of sleep experts, you will spend nearly one third of your life asleep. And while you slumber, your brain waves change as you move through the stages of sleep, and you will eventually arrive in a strange land known as REM sleep. The dreams that you have while in REM are often the most vivid and memorable.

In his book, *Why We Sleep*, professor of neuroscience and psychology Matthew Walker presents study after study that reveals the profound importance of REM sleep. According to his research, REM sleep, including dreams, provides a nightly dose of emotional release. In one study, two groups of subjects were shown an emotionally charged image twice, with twelve hours of rest in between. The control group saw the repeated image in the morning and at night, with no sleep in between. The experimental group also saw the same image, twelve hours apart, but with a full night of sleep in between. The sleep group reported a significant reduction in emotional charge when viewing the image for a second time; the nonsleep group, on the other hand, showed no reduction in emotional response to the imagery.

Other studies have shown the role REM sleep plays in creative problem solving and memory consolidation. Moreover, brain scanning technology has allowed researchers to better understand what goes on in the brain during REM sleep. We have learned that areas of the brain associated with visual and motor activity, as well as emotional and autobiographical memory, show increased activity during REM, while brain centers associated with rational thought essentially go offline.

DREAMS THAT CHANGED THE WORLD

Dreams are capable of much more than routine maintenance of the brain's cognitive and emotional functions. For those who allow themselves to tap into their full potential, dreams can be life changing. In his book *Our Dreaming Mind*, lifelong dream researcher Robert Van de Castle shares a multitude of stunning examples involving famous people who made life-changing discoveries as a result of their dreams.

From William Butler Yeats to Paul McCartney, countless artists, writers, and musicians have received direct inspiration for songs and poems from their dreams.

Dreams have also touched the lives of important leaders throughout history. Harriet Tubman reported that dreams showed her the safest routes for guiding slaves to safety along the Underground Railroad. As a result, she lost none of her "passengers."

Many a political figure has also had their hand guided by the messages contained in their dreams. President Lyndon B. Johnson was known to discuss his recurrent dreams with then White House aide and presidential historian Doris Kearns Goodwin; he would frequently awaken her to help him capture the content of his dreams while they were still fresh on his mind. At a time when Johnson was deeply troubled about America's involvement in the Vietnam War, racial unrest at home, and anguishing indecision about his political future, Johnson had a dream in which he was swimming in circles, unable to reach either bank of a river. Soon after this dream, he decided not to pursue reelection, a decision which may have been influenced by this and other significant dreams.

Dreams have also driven innovation. Perhaps one of the most astonishing accounts of this kind of inspiration from dreams is that of the famous Russian chemist Dmitri Mendeleev. Mendeleev was obsessed with the search for an organized system of the known elements of the universe. On February 17, 1869, after three days without sleep, he had the following dream: "I saw in a dream a table where all elements fell into place as required. Awakening, I immediately wrote it down on a piece of paper. Only in one place did a correction later seem necessary." Thus the periodic table of elements was formed.

As these examples clearly demonstrate, dreams contain the potential to reveal new information, inspire creativity, assist with problem solving, and offer sage guidance.

DREAM ANALYSIS IN PSYCHOTHERAPY

Dream analysis was once a central part of talk therapy. And to this day, the practice continues to be a central component of traditional psychoanalysis. Over time, with the growing popularity of cognitive behavioral therapy and other emerging modalities, the practice of dream analysis has fallen out of favor. And while contemporary theories and interventions have helped the profession of psychotherapy to mature, much wisdom is lost when we ignore the timeless power of dreams.

While dreamwork may seem esoteric, or even a waste of time to the pragmatic reader, the practice of dream journaling and dream analysis can provide tremendous benefits to your journey of self-discovery. It's not uncommon for people new to this process to see their dreams as profoundly strange and confusing. Some dreams are frightening and overwhelming, leaving you rattled throughout the day. Others can be delightful and pleasurable, allowing you a chance to enjoy fantastic and wonderful experiences.

When I was thirty, I had a fantastic dream of surfing on a sea of richly colored sand dunes while playing the bass guitar. Within days of this riveting dream, I got myself a bass, and I have enjoyed playing music ever since. I credit that dream for motivating me to take action on my desire to play music.

To better make sense of your dreams, it helps to have a framework including dream categories to consider. For starters, there are two broad categories to keep in mind: dreams to be explored and dreams to be ignored.

Dreams to be ignored include information processing dreams and traumatic flashback dreams. Flashback dreams are the painful reliving of actual traumatic events, while asleep. These dreams are typically a symptom of posttraumatic stress disorder and are not good candidates for analysis. As treatment progresses and PTSD symptoms improve, flashback dreams are likely to decrease in frequency. For those who remain haunted by nighttime flashbacks, there are some promising medications available to ameliorate symptoms. Research conducted by Murray Raskind has shown that Prazosin, a blood pressure medication, has proven effective in reducing the frequency of nightmares in patients with PTSD by lowering levels of noradrenaline (norepinephrine) in the brain.

The second kind of dream to be ignored is the so-called information processing dream. These dreams—a collage of images from the past day, devoid of story and emotional intensity—are most likely the brain's attempt to consolidate recent memories.

Dreams worthy of exploration (which, by the way, comprise the majority of dreams you will have) are those with both story and emotion. Such dreams are often vivid and surreal, ever-changing, and are frequently populated with a dynamic cast of characters. It's not uncommon for scenes to suddenly change—you are walking through your childhood neighborhood, then you are in an ancient city, now you are in a house. It's also not uncommon for people and objects to possess multiple, impossible qualities—you are talking to a man whose face you don't recognize and yet you know he's an old friend from college; he is also your cousin.

There are two primary ways to approach your dreams—objectively and subjectively. With an objective approach, people, places, and things in your dream are taken at face value. For example, if you dream about having a magical journey with your friend after having spent the day on a hike with her, then you may choose to view the dream through the lens of objective symbolism.

With a subjective approach, people, places, and things in your dreams represent aspects of yourself and your life. Thus, if you dream about a bear in the forest, a person trying to break into your house, or a delicious meal, each of those elements represents a part of yourself you are attempting to understand, express, and ultimately make peace with.

Much like art and literature, dreams often contain multiple layers of meaning. In *Mastering the Art of Psychotherapy*, therapist and author William Symes has described dreams as "illustrations of the dreamer's experience of the world and his or her emotional response to that experience." Symes proposes that dream imagery that is fearful and unfamiliar (tornadoes, forest fires, insects, reptiles, monsters, and hostile people) represent emotions and aspects of the unconscious that are more deeply repressed. Dream imagery that contains more acceptable characters and imagery (peaceful environments, friendly animals, familiar people) represent emotions and unconscious elements that are more integrated, and thus less of a threat to the conscious mind.

UNIVERSAL VERSUS PERSONAL MEANINGS

Your teeth crumbling and falling out, being chased, falling from a great height, appearing naked or half-dressed in public, repeating school classes that you are unprepared for, running late to the airport—these are all examples of common, recurring dreams.

While I would generally discourage you from consulting dream dictionaries, some dream symbols do appear to have universal meaning. For example, in many cases, houses represent feelings about the Self. As you become more self-aware, self-accepting, and otherwise on track with your life goals, the houses that show up in your dreams will likely become more welcoming, attractive, and easier to navigate. In addition to houses, other dream images often have universal, mythological significance.

The truth is, the majority of dream content is unique to the dreamer. The associations that you have with a particular person, place, animal, or object are more than likely connected to your personal history and your own symbol system. Making sense of it all can be quite the challenge. That's why it helps to record your dreams and discuss them with either your therapist or a dream group. If a dream doesn't make sense right away, don't be discouraged. Some dreams are elusive and others only make sense in hindsight. The important thing is that you are having a conversation with your unconscious mind and that you are making an effort to listen to the wisdom of your dreams.

ASK YOUR THERAPIST

Some therapists are not trained in dream analysis and thus don't have experience working with dreams. If this is the case with your therapist, ask them if they are willing to try to explore your dreams with you anyway. Some therapists interpret dreams according to a strict theoretical system, while others approach them more loosely, dealing with each one on an individualized basis. Regardless of approach, the important point is to have a conversation with yourself and create new associations, as you call upon your unconscious mind for support and guidance. Once this process has begun, the next step is to be on the lookout for recurring themes in your dreams. Progress can be seen through an evolution of your dream imagery, especially with regard to your recurrent dreams.

Getting started with dream work is simple:

- Get a journal, notebook, or some sort of recording device.
- Keep it on your nightstand or close to where you sleep.
- Write down your dream as soon as you wake up, no matter how trivial or strange, or fragmented—just write it down.
- Discuss your dreams with your therapist or consider joining a dream group.

Pro Tip: How to Better Remember Your Dreams

If you are having trouble remembering your dreams, try the following:

- Set an alarm to wake you up earlier than normal.
- Drink a full glass of water before bed.
- Before falling asleep, say to yourself, "I want to remember my dreams."
- It often helps to lie still for a few moments upon waking up; staying in the same position you were in while having your dream can aid in recalling more of a dream.

PART III

RELATIONSHIPS

"Knowing others is wisdom,
knowing yourself is enlightenment."

—Lao Tzu

Chapter Eighteen

Yourself: Finding Peace Within

Everything that you experience, everything that you do involves a relationship of some kind. Many relationships are obvious—your relationships with friends, family, neighbors, and coworkers. Other relationships are more subtle—your relationship with your body, with your mind, and with life in general. In this chapter, we will delve into your most fundamental relationship—your relationship to yourself.

As a result of my career path, I have had a lot of time to contemplate the human condition. The truth is, I feel incredibly lucky to be a therapist. I get paid to spend quality time with a diverse group of interesting people, at key inflection points in their lives. When people come to see me, they tend to be engaged and motivated; I get to meet my clients when life has their full attention. Given these opportunities for rich encounters with a wide variety of people, I've come to some conclusions about human nature.

YOU ARE UNIQUE—JUST LIKE EVERYBODY ELSE

One of the things that continues to amaze me is the fact that we are each so unique and yet so similar to each other. It's a bit like the way light is both a wave and a particle. We are unique insofar as we each have a story to tell. The particular combination of experiences—joys, heartbreaks, successes, failures, unforgettable moments—that you have had are completely specific to you; not even a twin brother or sister would have the same exact story to tell.

And yet, we share such a common humanity. We all struggle with the challenges of the body—getting sick, feeling pain, experiencing physical limitations of various kinds, old age (for most of us), and, ultimately, death. We all must navigate relationships with others as well as find a way to carve out a life in the world. And each of us must reckon with ourselves. That's right—whether you live in constant hiding from who you are, or you spend so much time in contemplation that you suffer from analysis-paralysis, no one can escape the existential task of forging some sort of relationship with ourselves.

RUNNING INTO YOURSELF

At the end of the day, when the work is done and the distractions are gone, you lie in bed with nothing but your breathing body and your wandering mind. Sooner or later, you catch up with yourself.

There is a reality show called *Alone* in which participants are dropped off on remote sections of Vancouver Island. These hardy individuals are tasked with surviving in the wilderness alone, with a limited number of items that they are allowed to bring with them. Many tap out early, due to fear, injury, or circumstantial problems. But the ones who last beyond the first several days all must reckon with themselves. The experience of being alone in nature tears away all of the familiar distractions and erodes defenses.

Watching the show, you can see these intrepid individuals wrestling with boredom and getting in touch with buried emotions, personal insecurities, and demons of the past laid bare by time spent alone. As I watched the participants cope with solitude, I was struck by an insight—we are so often afraid of facing ourselves, and yet we also deeply yearn to experience who we are at a deeper level. What a shame it would be to go through your whole life and never get to truly know yourself.

SLOW DOWN

If you are like most people, you live a hurried and busy life with more than your fair share of stress, stimulation, and distraction. To go a step further, chances are you rely on your busy lifestyle as a means of avoiding uncomfortable feelings. And yet, if you desire to better know yourself, you must learn to slow down, be still, and listen.

If you feel your blood pressure rising at the suggestion of slowing down, do not despair. You don't have to leave your family and join a monastery or meditate in a mountain cave for months on end in order to cultivate a deeper relationship with your psyche (although, for some people, extended retreats from daily life are just what the doctor ordered).

Cultivating a deeper relationship with your inner life can take a number of forms. Start simple, with one or two reasonable commitments to yourself:

- Create a journaling habit.
- Develop a meditation practice—you can start with five minutes a day and work up to longer sessions.
- Go on a weekly hike.
- Go on a ten-day media fast.
- Join a yoga class.
- Join a writers' group.
- Go on a spiritual retreat.
- Rediscover a favorite activity from your childhood.

Just as there are many paths to the summit of a mountain, there are many ways to deepen your relationship with yourself. Each of these practices is designed to help you to slow down and be more aware of your moment-by-moment experience. The important thing is to create new habits and rituals that allow you to pay attention to what is actually going on in your body, your mind, and your emotional life. In order for this kind of endeavor to succeed, a mindset of both curiosity and gentleness is paramount.

STAY IN YOUR LANE

Deepening your relationship with yourself will not only enhance your life, it can also improve your relationship to your significant other. In my work with couples, I frequently make the point that the fastest way to see changes in your relationship is to start by working on yourself.

It's tempting to try to change other people, to focus on what they could do differently to improve matters. But the truth is, real results come from focusing on your side of the street. Ultimately, the more you are at peace with yourself, the more effective you will be at addressing problems in your relationships with others.

DEEPER PARENTING

This concept also applies to parenthood. Anyone who has children knows how phenomenally challenging it is to raise a child. Feeling overwhelmed and in need of guidance, many parents head for the parenting section of the local bookstore. Once there, they find a sea of books, many of which are filled with techniques and strategies designed to produce positive parenting outcomes. And while many of these techniques are effective, meaningful change occurs only once the parent begins to work on themselves.

Let me give you an example. A parent who learns to better manage their own emotions is much more capable of responding to a high-conflict situation than one who has simply read a book and learned techniques, but not done the work on emotional regulation. To give another example, the parent who has not critically examined the way in which they were raised is bound to repeat cycles from their own childhood, either through conformity (raising their kids in the same manner they were raised) or rebellion (parenting the opposite of how they were raised). Both of these approaches lack the benefits of conscious self-reflection.

BALANCE

As we established in chapter 10, the psyche constantly seeks balance. And while for many of us, balance involves slowing down and learning to look within, there are some for whom the path toward balance is headed in the opposite direction. If you are the sort of person who has been in therapy for years on end, who has a small library of self-help books, who seeks self-improvement at every turn, then perhaps less focus upon the Self will help bring you into balance.

If this describes your relationship with yourself, then put down your journal and head out the door. Get involved with activities that get you out of your head, that utilize your body and find you engaged in dynamic actions. As always, there is no one-size-fits-all solution to life's challenges, including the challenge of a deeper, fuller relationship with yourself.

Whether your goal is to have a more fulfilling romantic relationship, or to have a healthier relationship with your parents, children, or friends, you must start within. As the writer and Buddhist teacher, Pema Chödrön once said, "Studying ourselves provides all the books we need." As you continue with your journey of therapy, consider discussing with your therapist which pathways toward greater self-awareness make sense for you. In the following chapter on parents, I will provide a road map for the next leg of the journey.

Chapter Nineteen

Family: "Tell me about your mother."

We all know the classic opening line of traditional psychoanalysis, as the title of this chapter denotes. And while, over time, the methods of therapy have changed, some things remain the same—if you are engaged in long-term therapy with goals that include transforming attitudes, behaviors, and relationship patterns, then you will need to spend some time discussing your family, especially your parents. This can include looking at pivotal experiences from the past, as well as present-day relationship dynamics, if your parents are still living.

The point of this endeavor is not to dredge up the past for its own sake, but rather to reach your full potential in the present. Let's face it: our past often lives on in the present, often outside of our awareness. ***Examining your early, formative relationships is one of the most powerful ways you can gain insight into how you approach current relationships with others.***

It does not take an advanced degree in psychology to know that we are shaped by our childhood experiences. And while much of our personalities are determined by genetics, that raw material is shaped by what happens along the way. While a complete discussion on the effects of childhood experiences on adult mental health is beyond the scope of this book, I do want to bring to your attention some key concepts that can accelerate your process of healing and change. If you wish, you can bring up these ideas with your therapist as they relate to your goals.

LITTLE "T" TRAUMA

The first concept for your consideration is the notion that we all experience some form of trauma during our developmental years. If you were abused or neglected, or if you grew up in a home with active addictions, or serious mental illness, this concept will be no surprise at all. But for those of you who had so-called happy childhoods, please pay close attention.

From time to time, my clients will report to me that they had loving and supportive parents, a stable home—end of story. What is implied is that nothing bad happened, so let's not waste any time discussing the past.

Unfortunately, it's not that simple. Even in stable, loving homes absent of abuse and neglect, there are stressful psychological forces at work. These stresses can take the form of environmental instability—frequent relocations, erratic schedules, feuding parents, chronic medical problems, undiagnosed mental illness, to name some common examples. Other stressors can take the form of psychological pressures. You can think of these forces as the unspoken, unwritten rules of family that are transmitted through silent contracts and tacit expectations. These forces exert psychological pressure, taking a toll on the developing personalities of children. Here are some examples of common expectations that exist within "normal" families:

- Boys are to be tough and independent; emotional sensitivity is not allowed.
- Girls are to be soft and cooperative; being angry is not allowed.
- Anger is inappropriate and should never be expressed.
- Expressing contrary opinions is rude.

- Children should anticipate and manage the moods of their parents.
- Sex is dirty and something to be ashamed of.
- The needs of others are more important than your own.
- Children are entitled to special treatment.

This is a small sampling of the psychological pressures that often exist within families. Each family has its own culture, with rules, rituals, and expectations that are transmitted from generation to generation. The daily, weekly, and yearly impact of these psychological stressors has been called by many names: conditioning, programming, little "t" trauma, to name a few.

Other examples of little "t" trauma that can shape your childhood include divorce, relocation, medical crises in the family, and other stressful events that fall outside of the boundaries of abuse and neglect. These types of experiences—and more importantly, how you learned to adapt to them—play a role in shaping how you function in your relationships now.

You might not have any memories of being treated badly. You may never have been abused or neglected. But you were shaped by your family, and the effect of that process leaves a legacy. Even the most mature, loving, well-intended parents make mistakes, applying pressure in ways that are stressful for the developing child. I have many friends who are fellow therapists. A handful of us started having kids around the same time. We would often joke about the fact that no matter what we do, we will all screw up our kids in one way or another. It's just a fact of life.

One of the best ways to bring these concepts to life is to focus on practical, present-day realities. Below is a series of questions designed to identify psychological blockages leftover from childhood conditioning. The answers to your questions will help you and your therapist to identify areas for further exploration.

- Are you able to think critically and develop your own opinions?
- Are you able to express yourself verbally, free of doubts, anxiety, or shame?

- Are you able to identify, feel, and express your emotions, or do you generally feel numb?
- Are you able to set boundaries, be assertive, and stand up for yourself with others?
- Are you able to enjoy sexual experiences, free of guilt, shame, and inhibition?
- Are you able to take care of your basic needs, such as maintaining personal safety, physical health, and financial stability?
- Are you able to identify and effectively pursue your life goals?

ASK YOUR THERAPIST

These are the fundamental questions you can utilize to diagnose areas of blockage that require attention. If you answered no to one or more questions, then discuss further with your therapist.

SURVIVAL SKILLS OF CHILDHOOD

As we have established, the traumas and challenges of childhood—regardless of whether they're big or small—leave their mark upon the developing psyche. As you grew up, you learned to cope with those challenges. Your unique blend of childhood coping skills are nothing short of survival strategies. In other words, you did what you had to do in order to make sense of and endure your environment, in circumstances largely out of your control.

Looking at this phenomenon from a bird's-eye view, two broad categories of adaptation emerge. The first category typically includes a combination of perfectionism, people pleasing, and conflict avoidance. The second category frequently consists of some combination of addictions, chronic lying, self-harm, and acting-out behaviors. Odds are, you either found yourself on the path of cooperation and *good* behavior or on the path of rebellion and *bad* behavior. Both strategies involve elements of self-preservation, and both strategies take their toll.

For many, the survival strategies developed in childhood persist to some degree into adulthood. And chances are, those coping patterns don't work as well as they used to. To be more specific, how you adapted to the stressful experiences at home and school almost certainly impacts your current relationships. Whether you are aware of it or not, those self-preservation strategies persist into adulthood, greatly influencing how you manage your relationships with others. If you want to transform yourself in the present and pave the way for the best possible future, you must understand your past.

An effective therapy experience will provide emotional support, structure, and guidance for exploring the issues described above. Together, you and your therapist can figure out exactly how far in-depth to go, as it relates to your therapeutic goals.

SOCIAL MODELING: THE GOOD, THE BAD, AND THE AWKWARD

For better or worse, your parents and caregivers are your most powerful and influential role models for how to be an adult. If you looked up to your folks, perhaps you now emulate them in some way. If you had a difficult relationship with your family, you may have vowed never to be anything like them. Most people fall somewhere in the middle, drawing on both good and bad memories from childhood. No matter what your experience of family was like, a blueprint for relationships and family life was presented to you in the form of your childhood experiences. Taking an honest and thorough look at the modeling you received is an essential part of becoming fully adult. Avoiding this process can result in either automatically behaving like your parents or automatically rejecting the gifts of your family.

RESISTANCE

Before we move on, I would like to acknowledge that some readers may find themselves resistant to critically examining their relationships with their parents. Such a feeling is both common and normal. Some of the most frequent barriers to discussing issues from childhood include these:

- Feeling protective of your parents, including the belief that discussing their flaws is disrespectful and disloyal
- Fearing that examining the topic will be painful and overwhelming
- Seeing no value in the endeavor
- Fearing that doing so will lead to dramatic changes in your present-day relationship with your parents

If these or any other concerns are present for you, talk it over with your therapist. A skillful therapist will be able to guide you in exploring your relationships with your parents in a way that is tailored to your needs and at a pace that is manageable for you.

Chapter Twenty

Lovers: The Eternal Quest for Companionship

The drive to connect intimately with another person is both primal and powerful. Biological, cultural, emotional, and perhaps even spiritual forces compel us to seek romantic partnerships.

Some of us are lucky enough to find love and keep it, with only a moderate degree of hardship. But for many others, the journey is fraught with peril—long periods of loneliness, ambivalent relationships, hurtful misunderstandings, painful conflicts, heartbreak, and divorce. When love relationships go awry, there is often a strong motivation to get help. Learning how to effectively navigate the demands of intimate relationships is one of the most common reasons people go into therapy.

While there is certainly no one-size-fits-all solution to relationship issues, some themes and patterns emerge. Over the course of this chapter, I will share my thoughts about how to sustain a healthy, intimate relationship. We will also take a look at what the experts say, and where they disagree.

RELATIONSHIP PROBLEMS COME IN ALL SHAPES AND SIZES

In my practice, I devote time to working with both couples and individuals. I've been pleased to discover that these two disciplines complement each other nicely. What I've learned as a marriage counselor has positively shaped how I view my individual clients with relationship issues, and vice versa. Here are some examples of common relationship problems that are addressed in therapy.

I once worked with a man in his forties who called my office seeking counseling because his wife was behaving erratically. He suspected that she was pulling away from him, possibly having an affair. He emphatically informed me he could come in at any time; he was willing to miss work at the logistics company where he was employed. Our sessions would frequently run overtime as he sought solace for his overwhelming anxiety, telling me story after story about the ongoing saga of his marital woes.

This pattern went on for several weeks, sometimes requiring two sessions per week. And then, just as quickly as the therapy began, it was over. The relationship was back on track and my client's anxiety was resolved. "I'll be back in touch if I ever need you again. Thanks for everything, Josh."

A recently retired business owner in her sixties came to see me because she was unhappy in her marriage. Her husband was kind and stable, but emotionally unavailable. They had grown children, many shared friends, a home they loved, and decades of history together. Her therapy involved learning to accept her husband's limitations, discovering ways to get her needs met from others in her life, and ultimately exploring the question of did she want to remain in her marriage.

Another client I treated for relationship issues, an attorney in her thirties, sought therapy with a goal of getting into a relationship. She badly wanted to meet someone compatible but was hampered by the painful memories of past relationships that had left her broken-hearted. Not only did she dread making herself vulnerable again, but the thought of returning to the dating scene filled her with anxiety. The longer she was single, the more she worried she would end up alone. Her therapy involved a focus on transforming her relationship patterns and developing clarity about what sort of partner she was looking for.

I have also worked with a variety of couples. One particularly fiery couple could not stop fighting, even when they were in my office. Both husband and wife had a compelling story for why they were *right* and, furthermore, why their grievances entitled them to their angry outbursts. If I let them go on without interruption, they would spend the entirety of each session replaying past arguments, at full volume. At times, I imagined myself wearing a referee's uniform, complete with a whistle between my teeth.

Another couple I treated didn't fight at all, and over time, they grew distant from each other. The few interests they shared were fraying at the edges. In my work with *hot couples*, like the first example, I frequently have to interrupt and redirect the discussion. In my work with *cool couples*, like the second example, the hour crawls by, with long silences filling the room.

As these examples illustrate, relationship challenges come in all shapes and sizes. While the details of your particular relationship issues will be unique, every relationship presents challenges of one kind or another. The good news is, most relationship problems respond favorably to therapy.

THE RULES OF LOVE KEEP CHANGING

In his book *The New Rules of Marriage*, Terrence Real makes the astute observation that couples today are attempting to navigate twenty-first-century relationships with twentieth-century skills. As a result, there exists a wide gap between what we expect from our relationships and the skills that we bring to the table.

In her groundbreaking work, author, international speaker, and clinician Esther Perel draws a similar conclusion, noting that today's romantics expect their partners to provide both security and adventure, novelty and predictability. In essence, they are looking to one person to fulfill the roles once provided by an entire community. This gap—the gap between what we want and what we have the ability to create—grows ever wider as cultural norms evolve, sometimes faster than folks can keep up with.

Given the seismic social changes that have occurred over the past six decades, it should come as no surprise that not all therapists agree on what constitutes a healthy relationship. Within the field of marriage counseling, there are a wide range of opinions on what members of a couple should be doing for each other and how marriage counseling should proceed. Some theories are oriented toward emotional security and attachment style while others emphasize communication skills, boundary setting, and taking responsibility for your own emotions. As is the case with individual therapists, some marriage counselors strictly adhere to a specific model while others draw on a blend of theories in their work with couples.

Thus far, we have established that (1) people want more from their romantic relationships than ever before; (2) higher expectations can only be met through the development of relationship skills and psychological maturity; (3) there is a breadth of opinions (even among the experts) regarding what constitutes a healthy relationship; and (4) cultural trends and social justice movements challenge long-standing assumptions and traditions. This can be a lot to digest.

ASK YOUR THERAPIST

Take comfort in knowing that a skillful therapist can serve as both an ambassador to the relevant information on the topic and a relationship coach. You might find it helpful to ask your therapist to share their thoughts about what makes a healthy relationship tick.

In the spirit of being both pragmatic and transparent, I will share my thoughts on the themes that I see most often in my work with couples.

ATTITUDE

An attitude of curiosity, flexibility, and open-mindedness goes a long way in relationships. If you take away only one point from this section, I want it to be this point. In chapter 9, I discussed moving from the mindset of "bad weather" to one of "appropriate clothing," and how profound that change in perspective can be. The realm of relationships provides a similar opportunity for a paradigm shift.

In relationships, the crucial pivot is from "being right" to "being relational." We all want to get our needs met, and often we also want to get our way. Getting your way could be as simple as choosing the restaurant on date night or the paint color for the living room. Or it could involve a monumental decision, such as where to live or whether or not to have kids.

When you and your partner don't agree on an issue, the desire to be understood can feel overwhelmingly powerful. In the heat of an argument, it can be tempting to double down on *why you are right and your partner is wrong*. The issue becomes black and white, win or lose. This mentality is your enemy. As Terrence Real often says, "You can be right or you can be married." Getting over the need to be right will prevent tremendous suffering. When you pivot toward curiosity and flexibility, you take important steps toward a win-win mentality. In a relationship, there is never a winner and a loser; there are either two winners or two losers.

Another crucial shift in attitude involves understanding and accepting differences. In his book, *Wired for Love*, Stan Tatkin catalogs many of the ways people function differently in relationships. From differences in attachment style to differences in how our brains work, humans are complicated and quirky. Some people think fast on their feet while others process slowly. Some people are great at reading facial expressions while others are clueless. Some people have a wide vocabulary for describing emotions, while others can't tell you how they are feeling.

The more you understand about yourself, your partner, and your differences, the better off you will be. Learning to be flexible and live with these differences can make sharing space a lot easier.

Let go of trying to change your partner and instead invest that energy into trying to better understand what makes them tick.

SKILLS

Enjoying a satisfying relationship—just like learning to play a musical instrument, practicing a sport, mastering a hobby, or anything worth accomplishing—requires the development of skills. And skills development requires practice. Foundational relationship skills include

- Articulation of needs, wants, and feelings,
- Boundary setting,
- Emotional regulation,
- Expression of empathy,
- Making sincere apologies,
- Repairing ruptures as quickly as possible,
- Active listening, and
- The ability to receive critical feedback.

Other important relationship skills include the adoption of specific rules and techniques to guide difficult conversations with your partner. In other words, you must learn how to argue without resorting to being mean, stubborn, or cruel.

Some relationship skills involve work you do on your own. This could mean addressing past trauma, developing greater emotional intelligence, and learning how to practice self-care. Other relationship skills involve how you relate to your partner. Listening with an open mind, remaining open-hearted even when you disagree with your partner, and developing the ability to compromise are skills worth developing.

Thankfully, there are more resources available today than ever before. From simple steps such as self-help books and web content, to more in-depth options like couples' retreats and intensives, a wealth of high-quality resources are available to you and your partner. As you will hear me say over and over again, there is no one-size-fits-all solution for relationship problems. Take a little time to shop around and get a feel for the people and ideas that resonate with you. And check out the Further Reading section at the end of the book to see my personal favorites.

When both you and your partner commit to learning and practicing relationship skills, you are likely to see real changes occur. Overcoming old patterns while developing new ways of relating can widen the possibilities for deeper love and greater connection between you and your partner.

ATTACHMENT STYLE

In the first two years of life, we each develop what mental health professionals call an attachment style. Your attachment style is a description of how you relate to your mother or other primary caregivers. Current attachment theories focus on how our early life relationship patterns influence the way that we relate to others as adults, especially our romantic partners. Having a basic understanding of your attachment profile—or relationship style—can help you to make sense of your relationship patterns, thus identifying areas for growth.

ASK YOUR THERAPIST

Ask your therapist to help you identify your relationship style, especially as it relates to your therapy goals.

RELATIONSHIPS GO THROUGH STAGES AND PHASES

Relationships, much like human beings, pass through developmental stages. Harville Hendrix, working with his wife, Helen LaKelly Hunt, identified three distinct stages of a relationship: (1) romantic love, (2) power struggle, and (3) conscious love. Sadly, many relationships don't make it to the third stage. Common outcomes of the second stage include

- Becoming a *hot couple* who frequently fight but remain together,
- Becoming a *cool couple* who drift into a relationship of separate but parallel lives (often for the sake of children or some other practical reason), or
- Ending the relationship.

Thankfully, these aren't the only ways the second stage can end. Relationships can move from power struggle to the establishment of a conscious relationship. Conscious love doesn't happen by accident. Creating this kind of union requires a certain level of sustained effort and commitment to personal growth. It can help to know that your power struggles are a normal part of being in a relationship, and that once the honeymoon phase has ended, there will inevitably be problems and differences to sort out.

Relationships also go through phases. Just like the rhythms of nature, our relationships also ebb and flow. Phases of greater closeness and harmony can be followed by phases of greater distance and conflict. Sadly, many people misinterpret a time of decreased connection as an indication that their relationship is doomed. If two people choose to live together for the duration of their adult lives, they are bound to go through changes.

Perhaps you or your partner will develop new hobbies, interests, or friendships at different times from each other—a development that can make the relationship feel unbalanced. One partner may pursue a career change or suffer the loss of a parent. Another common occurrence involves one partner going into therapy in the pursuit of personal growth, while their partner remains the same.

These are some common examples of changes that frequently create a phase of tension within a relationship. Just because the status quo has been disrupted does not mean that the relationship is over. Developing an appreciation for the waxing and waning of intimacy over time can help you remain patient and, more importantly, to remain in your marriage.

UNRESOLVED ISSUES, UNTREATED PROBLEMS

Untreated substance abuse, untreated mental illness, and unresolved trauma in one or both partners make maintaining a healthy relationship incredibly difficult. In fact, these problems are among the most common reasons relationships get off track.

Make no mistake, we all bring a certain amount of emotional baggage into our relationships. But if someone is involved in an active addiction process, has a serious mental illness that is not being treated, is engaged in acting-out behavior, or has significant trauma that has not been addressed in therapy, the relationship is sure to suffer.

If any of these problems are present, marriage counseling will be of little help until the individual(s) get into individual therapy and/or addictions treatment, and thus begin to actively address their issues in a meaningful way.

INFIDELITY

Affairs represent another source of significant relationship turmoil. While some betrayals are too severe to recover from, the majority of couples who face infidelity find a way to heal and stay together.

In some cases, an affair is the cause of the problem. In other cases, the affair is a symptom of a relationship already in trouble. If infidelity has struck your relationship, professional help may be required. Rebuilding trust and exploring what led to the affair are both essential to healing and moving forward.

In my work with both couples and individuals who have suffered from the aftermath of an affair, a common theme involves the willingness to stay with the relationship in spite of the betrayal. In the best of cases, partners can, over time, grow closer through the healing process. Such an outcome requires rigorous honesty, emotional sensitivity, and genuine efforts to repair the damage done. Working through the pain of the affair, including all of the difficult conversations required, can lead to a new, brighter chapter of your relationship.

RELATIONSHIPS AS A PATH OF GROWTH

At the end of the day, your views on the purpose of relationships will determine how deep your partnership with your beloved will be. If you see your relationship as simply a means to societal acceptance and financial security, your experience of intimacy will be severely limited. If you believe that your relationship can survive being on cruise control, while meanwhile your partner craves a deeper connection, you are in for a rude awakening.

On the other hand, if you view your relationship as a lifelong journey of shared discovery, and a catalyst for personal growth, you will surely experience the rewards of a deeper love.

Chapter Twenty-One

How to Date Smarter and Date Faster

SOMETIMES, I FEEL like a dating coach. As I write, I have at least half a dozen clients who are single and actively looking to get into a committed relationship. They are in their twenties, thirties, forties, and fifties. They are gay, straight, and bisexual. Some are divorced, some never married. All have been in love before and have been hurt by love too. We spend many a session analyzing dating interactions, discussing the development of new relationships, and ultimately exploring what it is that my clients are looking for.

RULES FOR DATING

If you are single with the goal of being in a relationship, I will give you the same advice I give to my clients:

- Make a list of what you are looking for in a partner. Include both qualities of the person and qualities you'd like the relationship to have. Be thorough. Include must-haves and deal breakers. Don't skimp. I personally find it helpful to break this list into five categories: personal characteristics, values, shared interests, relationship style, and overall stability.

- Don't waver on the important stuff. For example, if you want a partner who is financially stable, don't date someone who doesn't have a steady job. If you want someone who is kind, don't overlook the way they treat the wait staff.
- Be flexible on the little stuff. For example, get over your "type." Contrary to what you may believe, you can absolutely be attracted to someone who is shorter/taller, darker/lighter-skinned, or skinnier/curvier than you typically go for. This is not to say that attractiveness doesn't matter—it certainly does. It just means what you find attractive in the abstract and what you find attractive in real life might differ a bit.
- Date faster. How many relationships have you been through that, in hindsight, revealed hints of the fundamental problems on the first or second date? Trust your instincts and *stop giving people the benefit of the doubt*. You are not running a charity. If you can shorten the process from years to months, or from months to weeks, you will get to your person much faster and with less headache and heartbreak.
- Gather as much information as you possibly can, as quickly as you possibly can. In all seriousness, you are interviewing your date for the job of being your life partner. Your job is to find a way to gather intel while staying cool. Think James Bond or Veronica Mars. Do everything short of handing them a clipboard with a questionnaire. For fun, read *The Rosie Project* by Graeme Simsion. The protagonist—a geneticist with Asperger syndrome—actually gives prospective dates a questionnaire to fill out. (Spoiler alert—it doesn't go well.) It's a great read, full of heart and lots of laugh-out-loud moments.
- Consider the opinions of your friends and family. If you are head over heels with your new sweetie while everyone else in your life is giving you nervous looks, take that shit seriously.

- Be the person you want to be. If you are not comfortable with yourself, or with where you are in your life, you may not be ready to let someone else in. Part of you wants someone to share your life with and thus gets involved with other people. But if another part of you isn't ready, your unconscious will be slamming on the brakes, bringing your relationships to a screeching halt. You have to get your house in order before you can invite someone in to share it with you. Time and again, I have seen my clients find "the one" after reaching a significant personal achievement—becoming more assertive, getting their career on track, healing past trauma, and literally getting their house in order. In other words, if your quest to find someone else is a substitute for working on yourself, you will be forever disappointed with incompatible partners.

OVERCOMING THE ADDICTION TO FALLING IN LOVE

The single most important action you can do to improve your odds of having a stable, satisfying relationship is to be intentional about who you get involved with. My hope for you is that you will learn to approach the search for a partner in a more thoughtful, analytical way. I have become convinced that most people are allergic to approaching dating with the same logical rigor that they bring to any other major life decision (choosing a career, moving to a new city, buying a house). As a culture we are collectively addicted to the idea of falling in love.

But what is falling in love, exactly?

In many cases, it amounts to several months of being drunk on a cocktail of elevated hormones and neurotransmitters, combined with elaborate fantasies while getting lost in the excitement of a new person. It's only after the cascade of oxytocin, serotonin, and dopamine settles down that you can fully see the other person clearly. At this point you either (1) lucked out and your partner is compatible, (2) painfully came to terms with the fact that you need to end the relationship, or (3) talked yourself into staying with someone who is not a good match for you because you have already merged your lives to a degree that is difficult to dismantle.

Sadly, too many people find themselves in the latter two categories. Such an outcome is not inevitable, but you must be willing to radically revise your approach to dating in order to increase your odds of a better result.

THE NUMBERS GAME, REVISITED

Due to life circumstances, I have had the privilege of operating a private practice in two locations. I lived and worked in Fayetteville, Arkansas, for ten years before relocating to Albuquerque, New Mexico. The experience of practicing in two different communities has provided me with a rock-solid rebuttal to the frequent complaint that "there's just nobody to date where I live." Let me provide some context.

Fayetteville is a college town of about 85,000 people. By contrast, Albuquerque is midsize city with a population of around 550,000. In both places, many of my single clients have complained of the same thing: "The dating pool is too small. There's nobody out there that I don't already know. There are no good ones left." This sentiment is especially true in the gay and queer community. So imagine my joy and satisfaction when I watched client after client (both gay and straight) get into stable, committed relationships while working in Fayetteville.

Fast-forward to my move to New Mexico. I am rebuilding my practice and getting acquainted with a new city. It wasn't long before I began to hear the same refrain about the size of the dating pool being too small. As you can imagine, I chuckled to myself.

You can convince yourself that your community is too small, but unless you live in Hyder, Alaska; Slapout, Oklahoma; Derby Line, Vermont; or some other town with fewer than 500 people, you are deceiving yourself. The truth is, there is someone else out there who also badly wants to be in a relationship, who is also a bit frustrated and scared. Remember, it just takes one person.

DO THE THINGS YOU LOVE

Dating apps and websites allow you immediate access to other singles who are looking to connect. And while they are surely a central part of the quest for love in the twenty-first century, there is no substitute for pursuing your passions.

If you love the outdoors, join a meet-up group for day hikes. If you are a photographer, look for a photo club. If you like dancing, enroll in a dance class. The point is to pursue your passions while you are searching for love. Chances are, you might just meet a like-minded, self-motivated person who shares your love of bird watching, karaoke, or whatever activity that brings you together. And in the meantime, you will be doing things that you love.

IDENTIFYING YOUR PATTERNS

In addition to dating strategy, you may also want to take a thorough look at your relationship patterns. This includes both the characteristics of the people you get involved with and how you conduct yourself within your relationships. Many of the concepts covered in this book are designed to bring increased awareness and psychological flexibility to all areas of your life, especially the domain of relationships.

Your therapist will be able to guide you through the process of both identifying and transforming your relationship patterns.

PATIENCE WITH BEING SINGLE

The simple truth is if you want to find a partner who works for you, the capacity to be lonely is required. If you become impatient in your search for a partner, you may become vulnerable to getting involved with an inappropriate person out of loneliness, impatience, and desperation.

Most of us have done this at some point in our lives, many of us over and over again. The fact is, we are mammals, and we are wired to connect. We all want someone to cuddle up with, somebody to be our plus-one, someone to share the holidays with. But paradoxically, learning to wait for the right partner will help you get into the relationship you want faster. The alternative is to swerve in and out of unfulfilling relationships, each one requiring time for recovery and reflection before you can move on.

Of all the wonders and mysteries of life, relationships are one of the most fascinating and enigmatic. And while there is no universal formula for finding love, it is important to remain both persistent and flexible in your search for a mate. Chances are, they are just around the corner, eagerly looking for you too.

Chapter Twenty-Two

Conflict: It's Not as Bad as You Think

I FREQUENTLY TELL my clients that conflicts are like taxes—while nearly everyone dreads them, they are a fact of life. Just as ignoring your taxes will lead to both anxiety and a heap of trouble, avoiding conflict will ultimately do the same. Following this metaphor, you can deal with difficult issues a little bit at a time, as they come up, or you can pretend they don't exist as you accrue mounting debts in the form of resentment and tension—debts that will one day come due.

In this chapter, our focus will be on interpersonal conflicts with the important people in your life.

CONFLICT AVOIDANCE

In my years of practice, I have noticed that the majority of people who come in for therapy are conflict avoidant. I don't believe this is an accident, as the majority of people who come in for therapy are also either anxious, depressed, or both. These issues are often two sides of the same coin.

If you don't tell your partner how you feel when he interrupts you as you are sharing an important story from your day, you are repressing how you feel. If you are afraid to confront your office mate about the fact that they leave their dirty dishes in the sink for you to deal with, you are diminishing your energy. Do you bite your tongue when someone cruelly teases you, or tells an offensive joke, so as not to rock the boat?

If any of these examples sound familiar, you are conflict avoidant. And I will bet money that the sooner you start speaking up and telling the truth about how you feel, the sooner your anxiety and depression will begin to improve.

The two biggest obstacles to this interpersonal endeavor are guilt and fear. Most people who are conflict avoidant were controlled by guilt or threat of severe consequences in their family of origin. As a result, when you cross the invisible foul line discussed in chapter 15, you are likely to initially feel a surge of fear and guilt. The only remedy for this problem is repetition. Do the thing you fear. Over and over again.

THRIVING ON CONFLICT

A minority of my clients are comfortable with conflict. This happens as the result of being raised in a home where anger and conflict are commonplace, becoming rebellious in response to a repressive environment, or due to other temperamental factors.

Think of that friend of yours who loves a good debate, who tosses out controversial statements like chum in the water, just waiting for the feeding frenzy to begin. Or perhaps you know someone who never hesitates to tell you when they feel you have made a mistake.

If any of these examples sounds like you, this chapter will have something to offer you as well. If you struggle with impulsivity, often finding yourself in trouble due to your conflict style, you may want to read chapter 26 on anger. There is no single solution to issues with conflict. The goal is to identify your style and your limitations and then make a plan of action.

CONFLICT PATTERNS IN COUPLES

The majority of couples that I have worked with include one partner who is conflict avoidant and one partner who is an agitator. The person who is the agitator is frequently the one who calls me to set up therapy. A minority of couples will have two agitators; this couple will no doubt be a high-conflict couple, prone to screaming matches and other volatile incidents.

Also in the minority are couples where both parties are conflict avoidant. This is a breeding ground for psychological stagnation, passive-aggressive behaviors, and resentment.

No matter which category that you fall within, there are a few concepts that can make conflict resolution easier.

CALIBRATING YOUR THRESHOLDS

Inside each of us are two critical thresholds: the threshold of awareness and the threshold of expression. The *threshold of awareness* (TOA) is the point at which you become aware of a feeling or a need. This could be the moment you realize you are hungry or tired, as well as the moment when you realize you are feeling sad, hurt, or angry. These feelings can be directed toward a partner, friend, family member, or coworker.

No matter the circumstance, if your TOA is set too high, you will not recognize your needs and feelings until they are raging out of control. A simple example of this occurs when a person becomes "hangry," even though their hunger has been building up over the course of several hours. While getting some food in your belly is usually an easy fix, imagine the same problem in your relationship. If you have been unconsciously nursing a grudge for months about your girlfriend's tendency to be late, and your threshold of awareness only gets breached after the hundredth time, you may be in trouble. At this point, your response to her is likely to be out of proportion to the immediate problem.

In relationships, correctly calibrating your TOA plays an important role in keeping conflict manageable. The tools necessary for this job are curiosity, mindfulness, and permission to take your feelings seriously.

The *threshold of expression* (TOE) is the point at which you make your needs, wants, and feelings known to others. Some people have their threshold of awareness calibrated correctly; they know how they feel and what they want. But they may not allow themselves to speak up. If this is you, perhaps you silently judge others, imagining things you would like to say—if only you had the nerve. Or perhaps you convince yourself that things aren't so bad.

I once worked with a client who fantasized about leaving his husband once a zombie apocalypse occurred. This outrageous fantasy was as far as he was willing to let himself go in terms of acting on his feelings.

For some, both the TOA and the TOE are set too high. If this is the case, you don't identify your feelings and needs well, and once you do, you don't express them. This is a normal outcome for individuals who were raised in chaotic and unsupportive environments. It's as if you think to yourself, "This is as good as it gets." The belief that identifying and expressing your needs is a form of complaining and weakness can be another barrier to lowering your thresholds. Or perhaps you feel you do not deserve to be happy.

I once worked with a man who felt that his emotions weren't important. Life was about survival—making money and keeping your head above water. He believed that talking about feelings and making them a priority was a waste of time. In cases like these, therapy must focus on lowering both thresholds to an appropriate level.

ASK YOUR THERAPIST

Becoming effective at managing conflict starts with becoming aware of and adjusting these two key thresholds. Be sure to ask your therapist to help you assess and recalibrate your threshold of awareness and your threshold of expression.

ACCURACY OF EXPRESSION

A close cousin to the threshold of expression is the concept of *accuracy of emotional expression*. In most cases, if one person is upset with another, and the intensity of the emotional expression is in proportion to the problem, resolution can come rather easily.

Let's say that your friend forgets your birthday. You convey your disappointment, your friend apologizes, and you both move on. Now, let's say your friend forgets your birthday and you react by berating her, sobbing, and threatening to end the friendship. Here we have a real problem.

To take this idea even further, let's say that, as a child, your birthday was often forgotten. Now, as an adult, you react to your friend's mistake with emotional energy that belongs to someone else—your parents and everyone else who let you down in the past. To think of it quantitatively, 50 watt injury + 50 watt reaction = no problem, but 50 watt injury + 500 watt reaction = big problem! Those other 450 watts don't belong to your friend. Your friend will instinctively know that your reaction is out of proportion. And furthermore, your outsized reaction will not bring you any closure or healing. This is why you must always be vigilant, closely observing your reactions to situations.

If you notice that your emotional reactions are frequently out of proportion to the triggering event, it's time to ask yourself some probing questions. This type of behavior is an indication that there is some unfinished business from your past that requires attention. Don't hesitate to explore such topics with your therapist.

CONFLICT RESOLUTION TOOLKITS

So far we have discussed elements of conflict resolution that you can work on by yourself. The other half of effective conflict resolution involves the use of specific, deliberate communication methods utilized with another person. There are a great number of books and systems with formulas and prescriptions for skillfully resolving interpersonal conflict.

Nonviolent Communication (NVC), developed by Marshall Rosenberg, is a well-respected system that is grounded in limiting your expression of a problem to your needs and your feelings. Another helpful model for conflict resolution was developed by the Harvard Negotiation Project. Its philosophy and methods are outlined in *Difficult Conversations,* which presents some helpful concepts to guide you through conversations you need to have, but prefer to avoid. The book teaches readers to adopt a learning mindset and offers specific advice for listening more productively. It also breaks difficult conversations into three parts: (1) what happened, (2) feelings, and (3) what this means to me and my identity.

Most marriage counseling experts also have lots to say about successful conflict resolution. John and Julie Gottman, Stan Tatkin, Sue Johnson, and Terrence Real have all made critical contributions to the art of skillful and productive conflict resolution. Current theories utilize a blend of findings from neuroscience and attachment theory combined with hard-won clinical insights.

It has been my experience that, while structure helps, attitude is more important. In other words, *it matters less which system you decide to use, but rather that you commit to using a system.* And, more importantly, that you always seek to learn, grow, and look critically at yourself as you stretch beyond your comfort zone.

In closing, I would like to share that, when handled correctly, conflict can lead from breakdown to breakthrough. The emotional risks and honesty required for difficult discussions can often lead to healing conversations, encounters infused with deeper intimacy, greater understanding, and closeness between you and another. Just as the decaying underbrush of a forest makes great fertilizer for new plant growth, conflict can be the rich soil that gives rise to new growth within your relationships.

Chapter Twenty-Three

Estrangement: The End of the Road

Perhaps you are at a crossroads with someone in your life. Maybe you have spent countless hours talking about, fretting about, crying over, and even raging about this person. It could be a parent, a sibling, a friend, or someone else close to you. If you have been treated with cruelty and disregard, if you have been abused or neglected, if you feel as if you are constantly walking on eggshells around this person, you may be considering cutting this individual out of your life completely.

The decision to end a relationship with a close friend or family member can be absolutely heart-wrenching. In the most severe cases of abuse, the decision may actually be easier to make. When someone has deliberately hurt you over and over again, walking away without looking back becomes the obvious choice. But what about relationships that fall into a gray area? Those connections are the ones that often cause the greatest confusion.

Before the COVID-19 pandemic, I was in the process of forming a support group for clients who were struggling with difficult family members. The idea came to me when I realized I was having different versions of the same conversation with multiple clients. For one client, Sandy, therapy centered around learning to set boundaries with her narcissistic mother. Her mother was invasive, judgmental, and controlling—with no insight into her behavior. The arrival of Sandy's first child had forced the issue to the forefront.

With another client named Gill, therapy focused on unpacking his family's shared denial about the outrageous behavior of his older sister, who was self-destructive, unpredictable, and addicted to drugs. Her actions caused everyone around her tremendous suffering.

Meanwhile, another client of mine, Michelle, was deep in the throes of finding her voice and developing the courage to speak up to her controlling and verbally abusive older brother. In each case, the possibility of a full stop was on the table. Unfortunately, the pandemic prevented the group from forming, and so their work on these issues continued through individual therapy.

I found myself struck by how these three individuals—and so many other clients I have treated over the years—shared so many similarities in their stories. The ingredients are nearly always the same. There is either one parent or an entire family system that has a moderate-to-severe personality disorder. Having grown up around this person (or people) you may not have realized there was a problem, until you were older and began to compare notes with friends and lovers.

Having realized the problem, perhaps you made efforts to talk to this person about their actions, you attempted to set boundaries, and you tried any number of strategies to make the relationship more manageable. Perhaps this person is sometimes warm and generous, making the idea of hurting them seem unbearable. Furthermore, it's likely that you feel tremendous guilt when you attempt to make a confrontation or set a boundary. In some cases, this person is very well-liked by others in their community. Friends, coworkers, and neighbors who have not seen their mean, controlling, and volatile side may adore them.

The decision to cut someone out of your life forever is deeply personal. While your therapist cannot tell you what you should do, they can validate how you feel and give you a reality check about what healthy relationships are like.

It can also help to read accounts of others who have gone through something similar. Many of my clients have felt confused and isolated in their situation. Once they heard about others who had similar struggles with family members, they felt tremendous relief in knowing they were not alone.

There are many books that discuss methods of effective boundary setting, as well as other techniques for dealing with narcissistic parents, sociopaths in your midst, and other similar issues. If you have come to the end of the road with someone in your life, it can be helpful to have resources and support to help guide you toward skillful solutions for your situation.

Therapy often involves learning how to see the world accurately. Living with someone who is emotionally manipulative can skew your perception of what is true, what is fair, and what is healthy. Recalibrating both your perceptions and your nervous system can take a long time. That's why exploring issues of chronic abuse and severe relationship difficulty can become a central focus of therapy. In many cases, these issues go hand in hand with trauma therapy.

If you are facing issues of this nature, your therapist can become your ally in this work. Having a trusted and skilled guide will allow you to make progress on this most important journey.

PART IV

Issues Commonly Addressed in Therapy

"The only normal people are the ones you don't know very well."

—Alfred Adler, psychiatrist

Chapter Twenty-Four

Addictions

Addictions can take many forms: alcohol, drugs, gambling, sex, shopping, video games, social media, TV—you name it. Furthermore, the effects of addictions can range from mild distress to profound suffering, including broken relationships, chronic homelessness, and death.

Sadly, many who suffer from addictions do not get the help they need or continue to relapse in spite of resources and support. There is, however, much to be hopeful about. New discoveries about the brain continue to shed light on the neurological dynamics of addiction. Additionally, a host of new treatment approaches are emerging, providing a more holistic and robust set of options for individuals seeking treatment.

MANY TREATMENTS TO CHOOSE FROM

Historically, addiction treatment in the US has relied heavily on Alcoholics Anonymous (AA), Narcotics Anonymous (NA), and other 12-step programs as the go-to option. And while AA and NA are lifesaving and community-building organizations, there are many people who are unwilling to set foot in a 12-step meeting.

Thankfully, there are alternatives, such as SMART Recovery (Self-Management And Recovery Training), that are flexible, and based on the science of motivation as well as elements of cognitive behavioral therapy.

Whatever your addiction, whatever your personality type, treatment options are out there for you. There is no one-size-fits-all approach to getting sober and healthy. I have seen both clients and loved ones get sober, breaking the bonds of addictions in a variety of ways.

A CLOSER LOOK AT MILD-TO-MODERATE PROBLEMS

As with all mental health concerns, addictions exist on a continuum. As a result, individuals in the mild-to-moderate range are most vulnerable to both self-deception and underdiagnosis. It's very easy to tell yourself any number of stories that "prove" that you don't have a problem. Some common examples include these:

- "I can go weeks without drinking/smoking/using."
- "It doesn't interfere with my work."
- "I function better on weed."
- "I don't drink nearly as much as my friends do."

A more effective approach is to start asking yourself different questions:

- Do you ever have mixed feelings about your use?
- Have you ever tried to cut down and been unsuccessful?
- Do you ever wonder what life would be like without alcohol, drugs, pornography, and so forth?
- Does this behavior ever cause you problems, even if only occasionally?

When in doubt, talk it over with your therapist. Simply engaging in an honest, open dialogue with a spirit of curiosity can lead to positive changes.

APPROPRIATE LEVEL OF CARE

As previously noted, there is no universal approach to addictions treatment. That being said, the first issue to address is determining the appropriate level of care. Severe addictions typically require inpatient treatment. Getting off certain substances such as alcohol, benzodiazepines, and opioids requires close supervision by a medical team as well as a structured environment.

In less severe cases, addictions can be managed in an intensive outpatient program (IOP) or even with individual therapy (provided that the therapist has proper training in addiction recovery).

In my experience, addiction recovery is most successful when a holistic, multifaceted approach is used. Some of the most effective modalities and interventions used include

- Individual therapy focused on both underlying psychological issues and addictions recovery,
- Medication therapy,
- Group or social support, and
- Replacement behaviors and activities such as yoga, meditation, physical exercise, and creative pursuits.

With regard to medication therapy, drugs such as Naltrexone, Campral, and Suboxone reduce cravings for certain substances. These medications can be an essential component for patients who struggle with frequent relapse. In the case of addictions as self-medication for a mental illness, getting on the correct medication for your diagnosis is a key piece of the addiction puzzle.

Social support is another important piece of the puzzle. It can take the form of traditional groups (AA, NA), contemporary groups (SMART Recovery, Refuge Recovery, Celebrate Recovery), and online communities. Friends and family who are supportive of your sobriety can also play an important role.

Replacement behaviors and activities are also crucial to recovery. Always remember that, while destructive, addictive behaviors serve a purpose in one's life. Once the addiction is removed, something must be put in its place.

Chapter Twenty-Five

Attention-Deficit/ Hyperactivity Disorder

Attention-deficit/hyperactivity disorder (ADHD) is a neurological condition that is characterized by difficulty with executive functioning (planning, organization, emotional regulation, self-monitoring, time management, and self-control), a low threshold for boredom, and, in some cases, impulsivity.

TWO TYPES OF ADHD

ADHD (previously known as attention-deficit disorder or ADD) is subdivided into hyperactive and inattentive types. This means that, respectively, some with ADHD tend to be hyper and impulsive, while others are more inattentive and internally disorganized. This latter category is more common among females with the condition. As a matter of fact, women with ADHD often fly under the diagnostic radar, as gender roles can influence the way ADHD presents itself.

While children who get diagnosed with ADHD typically first show symptoms of hyperactivity and poor impulse control, adults who seek treatment for ADHD more often complain of difficulty with organization, time management, chronic procrastination, and motivation problems.

THE ROLE OF DEPRESSION AND LOW SELF-WORTH

Attention-deficit/hyperactivity disorder isn't just about focus; depression and low self-worth are common secondary symptoms. People with ADHD have typically struggled tremendously in school and employment settings. They have often been told that they need to calm down, focus, and get with the program. This combination of experiencing painful struggles in school and work, being the target of frequent criticism, and having the nagging feeling that "I'm just not living up to my full potential" can really take a toll on one's sense of Self.

The truth is, ADHD is not a disease to be cured, but rather a condition to be managed. In fact, there are some experts who challenge the notion that ADHD is a disorder.

THE UPSIDE OF ADHD

In his book, *The ADHD Advantage*, Dale Archer highlights the benefits of ADHD. Flipping the symptom profile around, Archer points out the strengths that many people with this condition have, such as "an ability to multitask, a propensity to thrive in situations of chaos; creative, nonlinear thinking; an adventurous spirit; a capacity for hyperfocus on something that fascinates you; resilience; high energy; a willingness to take calculated risks; and calmness under pressure." If you are able to effectively harness these qualities, you can experience unique advantages in life. On the other hand, without adequate structure, support, and education, living with ADHD can cause tremendous difficulty and distress.

While many think of ADHD as a relatively new diagnosis, the phenomenon has been documented for centuries. In ancient Greece, Hippocrates, the father of modern medicine, wrote about patients who had difficulty focusing on any one task and reacted with exceptional speed to things around them. Other physicians and educators have made similar observations over the years. Early terminology for the disorder included "nervous child" and "hyperkinetic reaction of childhood."

A BRIEF HISTORY OF ADHD

Modern psychiatry coined the term *ADD*, which was first introduced in 1980. It was later modified to ADHD in 1987. While originally considered a disorder of childhood that one will grow out of, it is now understood to be a lifelong condition.

Much controversy currently surrounds the diagnosis of ADHD, due largely to the aggressive marketing efforts of Big Pharma to medicate those with the condition. Beginning in the 1990s, widespread financial incentives for doctors to prescribe ADHD medications, combined with television ads targeted to frazzled educators and exhausted parents, led to an explosion of the diagnosis, especially in young children.

While some of this trend was clearly due to better assessment procedures, there was also a zeitgeist of labeling all hyper children as having the disorder. The unfortunate side effect of this was young children being overprescribed stimulant medication. While prescriptions for medication have arguably gotten out of control, for many with the disorder, medication is tremendously helpful, if not essential.

Richard Louv, author of *Last Child in the Woods*, has attempted to connect ADHD to what he has termed "nature-deficit disorder," the result of society's lack of connection to the natural world. While there is no empirical evidence to support the existence of nature-deficit disorder as a clinical syndrome, the concept bears further examination. As with any condition or disorder, there is always more to learn.

DIAGNOSIS AND TREATMENT

If you suspect that you may have ADHD, obtaining a proper diagnosis is key. Any licensed mental health professional can assess you for ADHD. In some cases, your therapist may refer you to a psychiatrist, psychologist, or neurologist who specializes in ADHD for further assessment and testing. Once an accurate diagnosis has been made, treatment can begin. Therapy for ADHD involves a combination of education, supportive counseling, mindfulness practice, and, in some cases, medication. In addition to traditional psychotherapy, individuals with ADHD may also benefit from working with a life coach.

If you have been diagnosed with ADHD, the first step is to learn as much as you can. Both *Driven to Distraction* and *The ADHD Advantage* are written by psychiatrists who themselves have ADHD. Both books are highly informative, accessible, compassionate, and practical in their approach.

The next step is to work with your therapist and other supportive people in your life to develop structure and habits that are tailored to your needs. Another aspect of your therapy may involve working through any difficult emotions associated with living with ADHD, including both past and present experiences that have caused distress.

Finally, it is important to note that, in many cases, ADHD presents unique challenges in relationships. It can be very helpful for your significant other and close relatives to become educated about the condition.

Chapter Twenty-Six

Anger

Anger is one of the six primary emotions originally identified by psychologist Paul Ekman (the others are happiness, sadness, fear, disgust, and surprise). Associated with the fight-or-flight response, anger performs a vital function. It indicates that something is wrong and then mobilizes the body to take action. But when anger is denied, repressed, or out of control, it is not serving its natural purpose, and destructive consequences are sure to follow.

A PRIMAL EMOTION

As overwhelming and mysterious as anger can be, humans have projected their anger onto the gods and goddesses for millennia. As a result, for many individuals, anger remains a wild beast that is poorly understood and resists all efforts to be tamed.

One of the biggest challenges in working with anger is finding an appropriate outlet for expression. To make matters worse, there are very few examples in the media of what a healthy expression of anger looks like. Thus, we are left with the task of being both courageous and creative in our efforts to develop a healthy relationship with anger. In this chapter, we will attempt to crack the code on anger management.

OVERT AND COVERT ANGER

Diagnosis of an anger management problem is simple—about half of the time. People with overt or explosive anger typically know they have a problem with their anger, or they have been given an ultimatum by a spouse or an employer. In some cases, these individuals have been court ordered to attend therapy.

On the other hand, many individuals express their anger in passive-aggressive and self-destructive ways. These individuals who manifest covert forms of anger are often completely unaware of their anger problems, which makes both assessment and treatment more difficult. A skilled therapist will be able to treat either form. For both overt and covert anger, the therapeutic goal is healthy assertiveness.

A MULTIFACETED APPROACH TO TREATMENT

Treatment for anger management can involve individual or group therapy, and in many cases, the combination of both is ideal. Group therapy can provide both peer support and accountability, while individual therapy allows individuals to go deeper into exploration of the stressors, emotional injuries, and other issues underlying their anger. I focus here on those strategies utilized in individual therapy.

Working with your anger in therapy typically involves a multifaceted approach. If your anger is of the overt and explosive variety, developing a practical toolkit will be essential. This involves such behavioral strategies as time-outs, deep breathing, and other activities designed to help calm the nervous system. It will also involve cognitive approaches designed to transform thoughts and beliefs that are contributing to unnecessary anger.

For example, excessive and chronic anger is nearly always fueled by irrational beliefs such as these:

- "This shouldn't be happening."
- "I'm being mistreated."
- "No one understands me."
- "This is completely unfair."

- "Why do I have such bad luck?"
- "I don't deserve this!"
- "This is bullshit!"

In addition to these cognitive behavioral approaches, therapy for anger nearly always involves getting in touch with the difficult emotions underlying your anger, such as grief, sadness, fear, as well as personal insecurities. Problematic anger is often the result of feeling out of control, or being unable to express other, pressing emotions.

Understanding what is going on inside the brain when a person feels flooded with anger can also make working on anger easier. Certain brain regions such as the amygdala become more active while others, such as the frontal lobe, tend to shut down.

For individuals with covert anger, therapy typically involves identification of needs, wants, and feelings. It can also involve overcoming conflict avoidance and developing assertiveness skills. Many individuals in this category are uncomfortable with anger—both their own and that of others—and thus must learn to tolerate anger and ultimately not feel overwhelmed by it.

As with individuals who suffer from explosive anger, people with covert anger problems will also need to explore past hurts, unexpressed emotions, and other issues that get to the root of the problem.

Chapter Twenty-Seven

Anxiety

Anxiety is both a fact of life and a normal part of the human condition. In fact, anxiety is at times useful; it is a powerful motivator where danger and deadlines are concerned. But when anxiety becomes either severe or persistent, and begins to take a toll on your mental well-being, it is time to seek professional help.

ANXIETY COMES IN MANY FORMS

Anxiety disorders that typically require psychological counseling include panic disorder, phobias, obsessive-compulsive disorder, posttraumatic stress disorder, social anxiety, and generalized anxiety disorder. In addition to people with these conditions, people who are overly anxious as a result of situational stress (relationship problems, work stress, interpersonal conflict, medical problems, and so forth) can also benefit from talking to a professional.

Regardless of how your anxiety tends to manifest, take comfort in knowing that anxiety disorders typically respond well to psychotherapy. As a matter of fact, anxiety is one of the most common reasons people seek mental health care.

In many cases, the issue of anxiety is further complicated by insomnia, depression, and substance abuse. According to some studies, individuals who suffer from an anxiety disorder are three times more likely to develop a substance abuse problem.

With proper help, however, all of these issues can be addressed and made more manageable. A wide variety of strategies and techniques can be learned and utilized to decrease the effects of anxiety. Your therapist can help you to better understand your anxiety and develop effective ways to both manage and transform its effect upon your life.

DECONSTRUCTING ANXIETY

One way to conceptualize anxiety is with the following formula: Energy + Information = Anxiety. This formula can help you unpack the reason for your anxiety, and then proceed accordingly. In my clinical practice, I have found it helpful for my clients to break down their anxiety, to dissect and analyze its causes. We begin with some questions and possible categories.

- First rule out any possible biological causes of anxiety. For example, excessive caffeine intake can lead to feeling anxious. Scheduling a physical examination with your primary healthcare provider to rule out any medical causes to your anxiety is always a wise first step.
- Is your anxiety connected to a real and present threat (an abusive relationship that you are presently in, past-due taxes, a global pandemic)? If your answer is yes, then determine the correct actions required to respond appropriately to the threat. You can thank your ancestors for passing on the ability to identify danger and live to fight another day.
- Is your anxiety connected to a historical danger (memories of abuse, being bullied, chaotic circumstances, war)? If the answer is yes, then you may be suffering from PTSD. In this case, therapy goals can include addressing and integrating those experiences. Part of this process involves the use of

reality checks. For example, asking simple questions such as, Is the thing that I am feeling anxious about present now? and How am I different now from who I was then, when the original trauma took place? In other words, reminding yourself of your present strengths, abilities, and resources. See chapter 43 for more information on trauma dynamics.

ASK YOUR THERAPIST

If the answer to all of the above questions is no, then you can begin to explore the possibility that you are suffering from conditioned anxiety. The majority of the concepts covered in part II of this book are designed to help you overcome the effects of conditioned emotional responses, including anxiety.

In many cases, anxiety is nothing more than energy in your body that your mind has mislabeled as something negative. This is especially true with novel situations. If you can learn to experience this energy as something neutral, or eventually as a positive experience, your attitude about it can begin to change.

The next time that you feel anxiety, take a moment to pay close attention to what you're actually feeling. Notice your thoughts, bodily sensations, emotions, and mental imagery. Keep in mind the possibility that you are simply labeling a higher energy state as anxiety. People often feel both anxious and excited before a big event or a new experience. Many a time, sensations associated with novelty and greater energy get mislabeled as anxiety.

Chapter Twenty-Eight

Autism and Asperger Syndrome

Autism, autism spectrum disorder (ASD), and Asperger syndrome all refer to a lifelong, neurological condition that impacts a person's social relationships, communication style, mental processing, and self-regulation, and is often accompanied by repetitive behaviors and narrow range of interests. Originally thought to be the result of poor parenting from "frigid mothers," autism is now understood to be a genetic condition. While much is still unknown about autism, the contributions to society by autistic people cannot be understated.

NEW TERMINOLOGY

Neurodiversity is a more contemporary term that provides a wider umbrella and nonpathological language for conceptualizing autism. Neurodiversity can be thought of as individual differences in brain function that occur naturally within the human population. Some include both ADHD and dyslexia within the scope of neurodiversity. Those who are not neurodiverse are referred to as neurotypical (that is, not having autism, ADHD, or dyslexia).

In his book *NeuroTribes*, Steve Silberman invites us to reconsider the notion of autism as a disease of childhood in need for a cure. If as a society we can learn to understand autism as a lifelong condition—full of both challenges and benefits—we will be in a much better position to improve the lives of autistic people. The more that we learn to honor and appreciate the unique talents and perspectives of neurodiverse people, the better off we will be.

UNIQUE CONTRIBUTIONS TO THE WORLD

Many of the brightest minds in the fields of music, medicine, engineering, mathematics, and physics belong to people who fall somewhere on the autism spectrum. Furthermore, many successful and talented entrepreneurs and entertainers have ADHD. These divergent "operating systems" contribute to unique ways of thinking, creating, and problem solving.

While autism is classified as a disorder in the *DSM-V*, a handbook used by mental health professionals to diagnose mental health issues, there is a movement among some experts and some autistic individuals to declassify it as a disorder. This movement is combined with an effort to reimagine language in such a way that autism is viewed as a form of naturally occurring individual differences. Advocates of this point of view reference the history of homosexuality's classification—and later dismissal—as a mental disorder by the profession of psychiatry.

Whether one views autism as a disorder or not, there is agreement that autism exists along a broad spectrum. The autism spectrum includes individuals who cannot speak as well as those who deliver acceptance speeches for the Nobel Prize.

GREATER ATTENTION ON AUTISM

Autism has received greater attention in recent years due to a combination of novel developments, including

- Changes in the diagnostic threshold for autism,
- Increased awareness of autism by clinicians, educators, and the general public,

- The *erroneous association* between vaccinations and autism (this is the result of a single, fraudulent study, that has since been discredited by the *Lancet*, the journal that originally published it, as well as by the scientific community as a whole),
- A wider offering of literature and resources on the topic, and
- Positive portrayals of autistic individuals in popular culture.

In my opinion we are not seeing an increase in the prevalence of autism but, rather, an increased awareness of it.

As a matter of fact, in my clinical practice, I am seeing more and more individuals who do not meet the full criteria for autism or Asperger syndrome, and yet demonstrate some traits or features of neurodiversity. These people have been here all along. In hindsight, my colleagues and I were viewing some of their issues through the wrong lenses.

Common examples of how these autistic traits show up in therapy include being unable to identify one's own emotions, difficulty reading and responding to the emotions of others, as well as obsessive interests. Many of these individuals are high-functioning professionals, often working as engineers, computer scientists, doctors, lawyers, academics, and law enforcement professionals. And while they are very successful professionally, these clients often run into thorny emotional and interpersonal challenges while attempting to navigate certain aspects of their relationships.

AUTISM IN RELATIONSHIPS

Over time, I have noticed a pattern involving one person's traits of neurodiversity becoming a central issue in relationship conflicts. For example, the neurotypical member of a couple becomes exasperated by his or her partner's inability to connect emotionally. The more that the frustrated neurotypical partner tries to get the neurodiverse significant other to work on the issue (often to no avail), the more the feeling of frustration grows.

In many of these cases, it has been my experience that the partner who has trouble connecting emotionally is often on the autism spectrum, but has not been formally diagnosed. In the majority of cases, this is because the degree of severity falls below a clinical threshold. You could say that the partner has "autism lite," is on the spectrum, or has mild autistic features. In situations like these, the hope that your partner will somehow change in core, fundamental ways is completely misguided and will only lead to further suffering.

Now, don't get me wrong—this does not mean that there is no room for behavioral changes and the development of new skills. But when one partner expects their significant other to be a different kind of person, to function in a way that is not compatible with their neurobiology, it will only lead to needless suffering for both members of the couple.

THERAPEUTIC GOALS AND STRATEGIES

Therapy for autistic individuals typically involves many of the same concerns addressed by neurotypical clients, concerns such as depression, social anxiety, loneliness, anger management, and relationship difficulties. Individuals with autism are less likely to be in a committed relationship and are thus more vulnerable to loneliness and social isolation. Furthermore, autistic individuals who are in relationships sometimes utilize therapy for guidance in identifying and expressing emotions and better understanding their partners.

The key difference in therapy for individuals with autism will be that the methods of treatment used will be more akin to teaching and coaching, and less based on emotional insight. Neurodiverse individuals typically learn and adopt new behaviors from memorizing concepts and applying them in specific, concrete ways.

Chapter Twenty-Nine

Bipolar Disorder

The word *bipolar* gets thrown around often, sometimes carelessly. We all have mood swings from time to time, and many of us know people who are particularly moody. But if you have bipolar disorder or someone you love does, you know that the condition involves more than everyday mood swings.

HIGH HIGHS AND LOW LOWS

The depths of the lows can leave a person stuck in bed for days or weeks, crippled with depression, unable to muster the willpower to do anything.

The highs of mania often start off with a pleasant burst of energy and free-flowing ideas. But before long, they can spiral out of control, leading in some cases to reckless spending sprees, risky sexual encounters, sleepless nights, and delusions of grandeur. For some patients, mania can also lead to psychosis—a combination of delusional thinking and a loss of contact with reality.

In less severe cases of bipolar disorder, episodes of depression and episodes of hypomania—a more controlled, shorter lasting form of mania—can still disrupt one's daily life, causing considerable emotional suffering.

Bipolar disorder affects approximately 1 percent of the adult population. In most cases, symptoms first appear during adolescence or early adulthood. And while the impact of bipolar disorder can be very significant, with an accurate diagnosis and proper treatment, the condition can be effectively managed, allowing you to enjoy life again.

A RANGE OF BIPOLAR CONDITIONS

Originally known as manic-depression, bipolar disorder is a neurological condition characterized by severe changes in mood, energy, and functionality. Bipolar disorder is typically subdivided into (1) Bipolar I (distinct depressive episodes and distinct manic episodes), (2) Bipolar II (depression and hypomania), and (3) Cyclothymia (rapidly cycling between depression and mania). It is worth noting that while for some, episodes of mania are euphoric, for many others, mania is marked by irritability and overwhelming, racing thoughts. Some clinicians view bipolar as a spectrum disorder, which may account for individuals who do not meet criteria for any of the categories listed above, but who manifest atypical forms of mood disturbance.

FAMOUS PEOPLE WITH BIPOLAR DISORDER

Many famous people, both living and deceased, have suffered from bipolar disorder. Looking back, it is very likely that Ludwig van Beethoven, Vincent van Gogh, Virginia Woolf, and Winston Churchill all suffered from the illness. In more recent history, Carrie Fisher, Jaco Pastorius, Demi Lovato, and Kanye West were all known to have been diagnosed with bipolar disorder. Given the prevalence of the condition among highly creative, innovative, and intelligent people, one may begin to wonder about the possible genetic correlation between bipolar disorder and higher IQ.

DIAGNOSIS AND TREATMENT

If you suspect that you have bipolar disorder, talk to your therapist about your concerns. They will most likely refer you to a psychiatrist or psychiatric provider for further assessment and treatment. As with any mental health condition, a proper diagnosis is essential. Bipolar disorder can often be misdiagnosed as unipolar depression, borderline personality disorder, and, in some cases, schizophrenia. Allowing a close friend or a family member to provide information to your mental health provider can aid in arriving at a correct diagnosis.

Once a diagnosis has been made, treatment can begin. As with many other illnesses, beginning treatment early can greatly improve outcomes with bipolar disorder. With each mood episode a person experiences, the brain undergoes a process known as kindling in which neurological pathways grow stronger. Like a car driving down a dirt road, day after day, electrical activity in the brain can create neurological grooves that become deeper over time. As a result, the earlier you begin treatment, the better that your outcome is likely to be.

Treatment for bipolar disorder typically involves a combination of medication, supportive psychotherapy, and IPSRT (interpersonal and social rhythm therapy). The purpose of IPSRT is to prevent mood episodes through the creation of stability in the patient's daily routine and in their interpersonal relationships. Regular, quality sleep combined with a consistent routine is essential for the successful management of bipolar disorder. Consistency helps to lower stress, thus decreasing the odds of triggering mood episodes.

Psychotherapy for clients with bipolar is in most cases supportive in nature, centered around the development and usage of effective coping and self-care skills. This form of therapy is typically not depth-oriented. Working with a therapist who is both knowledgeable about bipolar disorder and able to collaborate with your psychiatrist is of the utmost importance in securing a favorable outcome.

As researchers continue to learn more about the brain, novel insights about the causes of bipolar disorder are sure to emerge, along with continued improvements in available treatments options.

Chapter Thirty

Codependency

Codependency can be thought of as a recurrent, problematic relationship style that is characterized by poor boundaries, depleted sense of self-worth, and covertly self-destructive behaviors. Codependency can manifest in a myriad of ways—perfectionism, excessive caretaking of others, overdetermined sense of loyalty, controlling dynamics, to name a few. Underlying these problematic behaviors are either crippling emotions or emotional numbness. To make matters worse, codependency often goes unseen. A combination of self-deception and cooperative, high-functioning behavior allows codependency to fly under the radar

AN EVOLVING CONCEPT

The term *codependency* was originally coined to describe the partner of an alcoholic or a drug addict. Since this phenomenon was originally identified, the definition of codependency has expanded to include individuals who suffer from a wider variety of self-destructive relationship patterns.

While it is often thought of in the context of marital relationships, a person can behave codependently with friends, coworkers, and other family members. Regardless of the context, the core structural features are the same:

- Developmental trauma (abuse, neglect, inconsistent parenting, or environmental chaos that occurs during key developmental periods)
- Distorted sense of Self
- Poor boundaries, both physically and psychologically
- Excessive caretaking and/or controlling behavior
- Devaluation of one's own needs and wants
- Distorted emotional life (this can include overwhelming emotions or emotional numbness)
- In extreme cases, a complete inability to register one's own needs and wants

Not surprisingly, codependency frequently overlaps with other problems such as depression, anxiety, and posttraumatic stress disorder.

THERAPEUTIC STRATEGIES

Therapy for the treatment of codependency is often a long-term process. One of the biggest challenges in therapy can be an overdetermined or premature focus on encouraging the codependent client to leave a toxic relationship. Obviously, in the case of severe abuse, where the individual's health and safety are in jeopardy, finding the safest possible exit is the first order of business. But in most other cases, helping the codependent person to leave a relationship without addressing the underlying issues is the same as moving to a new city and expecting your problems to stay behind. The chances that you will find yourself in another codependent relationship can sadly be quite high.

As a result, therapy must focus on (1) identifying and addressing past trauma, (2) transforming thoughts and beliefs about the Self, (3) identifying and expressing feelings, needs, and wants, and (4) learning to set and maintain boundaries. Once the individual can begin to make real changes in their current relationship, then they can explore the possibility of moving on, if so desired.

In addition to individual therapy, many people suffering from codependency have also found great benefit from group work, including 12-step programs such as Codependents Anonymous (CoDA) and others. A wide variety of resources exists to help people suffering from codependency develop the skills and attitudes necessary to lead a more functional, satisfying, and empowered life.

Chapter Thirty-One

Depression

Everyone gets sad from time to time. As one of the six primary emotions, sadness is the natural response to loss, disappointment, and other forms of adversity. Even though depression, sadness, and the blues get lumped together, they are not the same thing.

MORE THAN THE BLUES

Clinical depression can take many forms. These include major depressive disorder, pervasive depressive disorder (formerly known as dysthymia), psychotic depression, and seasonal affective disorder. Depression is also a major component of bipolar disorder, which involves a combination of depressive episodes and mania.

In practical terms, depression goes well beyond sadness, often manifesting in some or all of the following symptoms:

- Loss of energy
- Depressed mood
- Decreased motivation
- Difficulty concentrating

- Distorted, self-critical thinking
- Changes in appetite
- Changes in sleep patterns
- Decreased sex drive
- Inability to experience pleasure
- Thoughts of death, including suicidal ideation

Depressive episodes can last anywhere from a couple of weeks, to months at a time. Some individuals go in and out of depressive episodes, while others suffer from chronic depression, a condition that can last for years. No matter how depression manifests itself, it has the power to suck the joy and color out of life, taking a toll on both career and relationships, while causing profound emotional suffering.

CAUSES OF DEPRESSION

As with most mental health concerns, depression can be caused by a combination of situational, psychological, and biological factors. A family history of depression or bipolar disorder is a risk factor for clinical depression. Additionally, certain personality configurations appear to be more prone to depression. These can include individuals with a personality disorder, as well as individuals with a pessimistic outlook.

Clinical depression can also emerge during or following a period of prolonged situational stress, including divorce, death of a loved one, job loss, or chronic pain. And sadly, it is not uncommon for a depressed person to experience all of the above simultaneously, exacerbating the condition. Finally, depression often accompanies other mental health problems, most notably anxiety, PTSD, and substance abuse.

It is important to understand that in many cases, depression is the result of unexpressed emotions. Anger, sadness, fear, and grief—when blocked, ignored, and buried in the unconscious—can come back in the form of depressed mood. The energy of these natural emotions becomes stuck inside the unconscious mind. Therapy involves the liberation of this repressed emotional energy through exploration, identification, and expression.

As with blocked emotions, unfulfilled purpose can also lead to depression. If an important part of yourself has been abandoned or ignored (creative expression, living according to your values, important career ambitions, service to others, spiritual development), depression can result.

THE ROLE OF GENDER IN DEPRESSION

Interestingly, depression frequently manifests differently for men than it does for women. Many women diagnosed with depression exhibit the classic symptoms listed above. But many men—especially those socialized to be strong, and independent—exhibit what we call covert depression. Covert depression among men is explored in Terrence Real's book, *I Don't Want to Talk About It.* Real explains that for men, depression can show up as chronic anger and irritability, substance abuse, sex and love addiction, workaholism, and other similar manifestations. In other words, men and women sometimes express depression in ways that are culturally sanctioned for their gender.

A RANGE OF TREATMENT OPTIONS

Treatment for depression often includes a combination of therapies and modalities. In my practice, I do not consider a referral for medication management until at least six months of individual therapy has been completed. I do, however, make exceptions for suicidal patients or when someone is suffering from overwhelming symptoms. If there is no improvement in mood after six months of therapy, a psychiatric consultation may be in order.

In most cases of mild to moderate depression, you can expect to see significant improvement with a combination of therapy and habit changes such as physical exercise, meditation, social activity, and time spent in nature. For people with moderate to severe depression, a combination of psychotherapy and medication is often most effective. And for those who suffer from treatment-resistant depression, a more aggressive and comprehensive treatment plan is often required. This can include both a more in-depth assessment as well as a broader range of therapies.

Chapter Thirty-Two

Difficult People

Don Draper, Walter White, Claire Underwood. These characters have one thing in common—they create problems for everyone else. Difficult people are the ones we love to talk about when they are not around. Difficult people become the focus of our attention not only because they are a pain in the ass, but also because we so desperately want to understand them. Why do they do the things they do? How can they get away with such outrageous behavior? These are just some of the questions that can leave you feeling puzzled and frazzled.

If you are seeking therapy because of a difficult relationship, chances are you are at your wit's end with someone in your life. It could be a boss, a parent, a friend, or a neighbor. Let's face it, some relationships are so trying that you may feel compelled to seek professional help in order to deal with them. In such cases, a therapist can provide emotional support, strategic suggestions, skills building, and psychoeducation.

THE IMPACT OF PERSONALITY DISORDERS

Psychoeducation typically involves a discussion of personality disorders, with your therapist educating you on the basics of the topic. For the majority of the cases I have worked on involving severe relationship problems with a loved one, the person in question suffered from one of three personality disorders—antisocial personality disorder (psychopaths and sociopaths), narcissistic personality disorder (NPD), and borderline personality disorder (BPD). For many clients, coming to a deeper understanding of the psychology of the person (or people) they are having problems with is profoundly liberating.

SKILLS DEVELOPMENT

Therapy for dealing with difficult people frequently involves skills development. Assertiveness, boundary setting, boundary maintenance, and self-care are all critical skills to have. Your therapist can role-play difficult conversations with you, helping you prepare for upcoming encounters and to better manage ongoing relationship dynamics.

If you were raised in a family that was abusive, that chronically invalidated your experience, or was otherwise chaotic, you may be susceptible to discounting your feelings and doubting your perception of reality. This is especially true when it comes to relationships with difficult people. Typical distortions of belief include the notion that your feelings don't matter, and attempts to convince yourself that "it's not that bad." Your therapist can give you a reality check and can encourage you to take your own feelings, instincts, and judgment calls seriously.

In some situations, the solution to problems with difficult people is to end the relationship altogether. See chapter 23, for more thoughts on the matter. In other cases, cutting off a relationship with a difficult person may not be a realistic option. Whatever your goal, your therapist can help you navigate the turbulent waters of relationships with difficult people.

Chapter Thirty-Three

Grief and Loss

The death of a loved one can send the strongest person into a tailspin of grief and depression. Losing someone dear to you leaves an empty space, a void filled with painful emotions.

In addition to the raw pain of loss, when someone you love dies, you may find yourself thrust into new and unfamiliar roles. For example, if you have lost your spouse, you may find yourself needing to take on daily tasks and responsibilities that previously belonged to them. Or perhaps you have lost a prominent person in your family or organization. Their absence leaves others scrambling to fill their shoes. These kinds of changes can feel overwhelming. But talking to a professional can help make the pain more bearable.

SUPPORTIVE THERAPY AND BEYOND

Therapy for grief and loss typically falls under the category of supportive therapy. Therapy of this kind involves a lot of listening, empathy, and, quite often, tears. Your therapist can provide comfort, helping you find your way through a difficult time.

Everybody grieves in different ways, and your therapist will be able to respect your unique path. And just as people grieve differently, there is not a standard time line for mourning a loss. While we may speak of moving on, there are certain losses that we never get over. Some people are such a central part of our lives that we will always be affected by their absence.

Instances of loss that involve complicated grief call for more in-depth therapy. This is the case when the cause of death was traumatic or untimely, or when the relationship with the deceased was complicated by abuse, neglect, or was otherwise strained. And finally, if grief or loss has activated depression, anxiety, or another mental health issue, therapy will involve the additional components necessary to help you address those concerns.

LOSS CAN TAKE MANY FORMS

It's worth noting that loss can take many forms, besides the death of a loved one. Over the course of life, we are all prone to suffer losses, both great and small. We lose intangibles such as innocence and freedom, as well as relationships, physical abilities, jobs, places, and possessions. Each of these experiences can take a toll. Whatever form loss takes, a wound can be left behind, in need of care. Getting professional help can accelerate your process of healing while offering additional support during your time of grief.

Chapter Thirty-Four

Guilt and Shame

Though it gets a bad rap, guilt performs a useful psychological function, as long as it is not contaminated. The emotion of guilt is appropriate when it results from violating your own values. For example, if you lose your temper and scream at your partner, then feeling guilty is an appropriate response. In this case, your guilt is your conscience talking to you, letting you know that you behaved harshly. The feeling can motivate you to (1) repair the damage done and (2) take action to prevent further problems in the future.

CONDITIONED GUILT

If, however, you feel guilty when you engage in healthy behaviors such as boundary setting and civil disagreements, then you are experiencing conditioned guilt. This form of guilt is a problem. In this scenario, conditioned guilt would most likely be the result of being raised in a family that discouraged the expression of contrary opinions or that taught you to defer to the will of others. In other words, conditioned guilt is the result of *violating someone else's values*, not your own.

Many of us unconsciously internalize the values of our primary caregivers and are thus unaware of the origins of our guilty feelings. This corrupted expression of guilt can be quite harmful because not only does it cause you to suffer, it also interferes with your ability to be genuine. If this kind of guilt shows up regularly in your life, this should become a topic for discussion with your therapist.

CONFUSING GUILT WITH COMPASSION

Another common pattern that I see my clients struggle with in regard to this issue occurs when guilt and compassion become confused. I frequently hear my clients report feeling guilty about troubles someone else in their life is going through. In these cases, my client is not responsible for the pain and suffering that their loved one is experiencing, and yet they feel guilty about the gap between their own reality and the state of suffering of another. In situations like these, you are feeling compassion for someone who suffers combined with some version of "survivor's guilt" at having a better circumstance in life. The solution to this problem is to take the guilt out of the equation, as it does not do a thing to help anyone else. Instead, go deeper into your feelings of compassion. They just might guide you toward a way of helping someone who is hurting, and meanwhile you will be freed of an unnecessary burden.

IN THE SHADOW OF SHAME

A first cousin of guilt, shame has gotten a lot of attention recently due to the groundbreaking work of author and researcher Brené Brown who has made her career researching vulnerability, courage, shame, and empathy. Brown's work on the impact shame has on one's identity and psychological well-being is truly worth exploring.

According to Brown, shame is a destructive emotion associated with core, negative beliefs about your self-worth and your ability to be loved. Shame is associated with higher rates of depression, substance abuse, and other psychological problems. Overcoming shame involves learning to detach from perfectionism, developing the capacity to be psychologically vulnerable, and letting go of the many defense mechanisms and emotional armoring that many, if not all, of us use to mitigate our insecurities.

Whether you suffer from conditioned guilt, toxic shame, or a combination of the two, therapy can help you to regain emotional balance and to enjoy your experience of life without feeling bad for being yourself and doing the things you want to do.

Chapter Thirty-Five

Life Transitions

Moving to a new city, leaving home for the first time, changing careers, getting married, getting divorced, the birth of a child, the empty nest, retirement—these are just some of the major life transitions that can lead a person to seek counseling.

Life transitions, both positive and negative, are often a source of significant stress, and sometimes the stress of change is too much to handle on your own. Many people go into counseling for the first time to get help managing stress brought on by these pivotal life chapters.

SOLUTION-ORIENTED THERAPY

Therapy for these kinds of issues is often short term and solution oriented. You may be going through a stressful time and find yourself in need of emotional support and better coping skills. A therapist can provide you with empathy and a fresh perspective on your situation; they can also help you develop enhanced skills for self-care and stress management. In many cases, therapy will draw to a close once you have adapted to the changes at hand and feel more capable of dealing with stress on your own.

GOING DEEPER

Alternately, some people who enter therapy to deal with a life transition decide—after having forged a positive relationship with a therapist and enjoying the benefits of counseling—to continue with long-term psychotherapy after their initial goals have been met. You may be curious about your inner life and wish to learn more about yourself. Or perhaps you have unfulfilled potential that you want to explore and develop.

It's also common for therapy to uncover old wounds in need of healing. Periodically reviewing progress and reconsidering goals will help keep your therapy on track and provide opportunity for new areas of growth to emerge.

Transitions are a part of life, no matter who you are. While they can be stressful to the extent that they are outwardly disruptive and challenge your sense of identity, they can also provide profound opportunities for growth and evolution. As Richard Bach so beautifully put it, "What the caterpillar calls the end of the world, the master calls a butterfly."

Chapter Thirty-Six

Obsessive-Compulsive Disorder

Approximately 1 to 2 percent of adults will meet criteria for OCD at any given time. A typical treatment plan involves a combination of therapy and medication. If you think you may suffer from OCD, ask your therapist to conduct an assessment and consider asking for a referral to a psychiatrist.

THE DOUBTING DISEASE

Obsessive-compulsive disorder (OCD) was described as religious melancholy as early as the seventeenth century. Its ill effects were observed even further back, notably in the writings and reports of Martin Luther. Luther was notorious for making painfully long confessions in which he would detail a litany of impure thoughts and perceived transgressions to a beleaguered priest.

This is the nature of OCD. This so-called doubting disease involves, among other things, a fear of your own thoughts. Those who live with this largely neurological illness are afflicted with obsessive thoughts that lead to significant anxiety and distress. Obsessive thoughts are typically organized around themes, including

- Germs, illness, and contamination,
- Sexual shame,
- Religious motifs, or
- Counting and symmetry.

In an effort to mitigate the anxiety associated with obsessive thoughts, compulsive rituals are often utilized. Examples include lengthy handwashing rituals that, in extreme cases, devolve into the use of bleach or other harsh chemicals. Other compulsive rituals include repeatedly checking that doors are locked and the stove is turned off.

In some cases, the compulsions can be mental activities, including visualizing certain images, counting rituals, and prayers. I once heard a story about a man with OCD who, whenever he felt a bump in the road, became convinced that he had accidentally run over a pedestrian. As a result, he would drive back to where he hit the bump, sometimes multiple times, causing him to be late for work.

While many people have a touch of OCD traits (a need for order, occasionally going back to check if the door is locked for a second time), those who have the diagnosis of OCD often spend an hour or more per day obeying their routines and rituals. Given the high levels of distress that come with the disorder, it is not uncommon for individuals with OCD to also suffer from clinical depression.

FACING YOUR FEARS

Travel writer and naturalist Jeremy Hance opens up about his struggles with OCD in his recent memoir, *Baggage: Tales of a Globe-Trotting Hypochondriac*. Hance shares openly about his overwhelming fears of germs, disease, and illness, sometimes going so far as to consult multiple doctors, even after receiving a clean bill of health.

Though OCD causes Hance tremendous suffering and presents significant obstacles with regard to travel, he courageously marches forward. He ventures deep into the Amazon jungle and goes on an African safari, repeatedly placing himself in environments that put his psychological limits to the test. Hance's memoir is an example of an effective response to OCD, a form of self-directed exposure therapy. In other words, the best way to deal with OCD is to face the things you fear. With repeated exposure, you increase your distress tolerance and lower your anxiety. This will make it possible to participate in life more fully and with greater confidence.

Chapter Thirty-Seven

Parenting Concerns

Raising children is one of the hardest jobs in the world. And to make matters worse, the sheer volume of parenting advice can feel deafening. When the task of parenting becomes overwhelming and unmanageable, it's time to seek professional help.

Therapy for parenting concerns can be brief and solution oriented, or long term and in depth. In either case, your therapist can assist you with exploring your concerns, reaching your goals, and, ultimately, cultivating an improved relationship with your offspring.

When approaching parenting concerns, it is helpful to consider four categories: (1) relationship health, (2) strategy and technique, (3) managing your own emotions, and (4) addressing your past.

RELATIONSHIP HEALTH

The best techniques in the world aren't worth a hill of beans if you don't have a loving relationship with your child. Children are motivated to cooperate out of respect and a genuine desire to please, not by fear or bribes.

When the relationship between parent and child is damaged, either through fear or neglect, your credibility and leverage are severely limited. The quality of your relationship is determined by a lifetime of shared experiences, so the sooner you make adjustments, the better.

Building a healthy relationship with your children requires your undivided attention and an open mind. You have to be able to enter their world, to try to see life through their eyes. It can help to literally get down on the ground and view the environment from your child's vantage point. It involves playing with them, learning the characters and stories that occupy their imagination, and, above all, creating shared, meaningful experiences. Not only will this increase the odds of your child cooperating with you, it will lead to a more rewarding relationship for you both.

STRATEGY

Strategy and technique depend on your child's current developmental stage, their temperament, and the issues at hand. The Love and Logic series of books (for early childhood) does a fine job of showcasing the power of empathy combined with behavioral consequences in a format that is fairly easy to use. Many other books also offer strategies and effective techniques for child rearing and behavioral management.

Broadly speaking, it is best if you can start early. Waiting until you have a surly teenager on your hands to develop your parenting strategy is a recipe for disaster. Being consistent is also key. It takes time for both parent and child to adjust to new rules and expectations, but if you stick with a plan, it will eventually pay off.

Strategies that don't work include lectures, threats, yelling, and spanking. Do not be fooled. While some of these techniques will work in the short term—shocking your child into compliance—these approaches will backfire in the long run. Studies consistently show that spanking and other forms of harsh discipline lead to increased aggression, antisocial behavior, and mental health problems in later life. Additionally, authoritarian parenting approaches are sure to undermine the relationship between you and your child.

EMOTIONAL REGULATION

Every parent knows that, sooner or later, your kids will push your buttons. That's why one of the most helpful things you can do as a parent is to develop a practice for managing your own emotions. Gaining control of your emotional reactions pays huge dividends. You will be able to minimize regrettable instances of losing your temper, maximize creative problem solving, and, most importantly, role-model how to manage difficult feelings.

If you struggle with losing your temper and have poor impulse control, you will need to develop an anger action plan. This will include a specific set of things you do when triggered, including taking a time-out for yourself. You may find that it helps to visualize and rehearse what you plan to do when things get heated. I like to think of this as a mental fire drill for anger. Taking twenty minutes away from an overwhelming situation, doing some deep breathing, remembering your values, and thinking through how best to respond to your child will help you get out of the primitive, reactive parts of your brain and back into a compassionate, problem-solving mindset.

Developing this skill set takes practice. Just like anything else in life worth having, you will get back out of it exactly as much as you put into it.

ADDRESSING YOUR PAST

A crucial component of becoming the parent you aspire to be involves taking an honest look at how you were raised. Without an examination of your past, how can you hope to create a better future? See chapter 19 for more on this topic.

Whatever your parenting concerns may be, therapy can help you to develop the emotional insight and behavioral tools necessary for working toward your goals.

Chapter Thirty-Eight

Personality Disorders

Like most mental health issues, personality disorders exist on a spectrum. Regardless of how serious your personality issues are, the central goal is to increase your mental and emotional flexibility. Doing so will allow for better self-care and a greater range of skillful behaviors. By the same token, the more rigid your point of view is, the more you are likely to suffer.

A BRIEF HISTORY

Philosophers, physicians, and psychologists have studied the nuances and complexities of personality structure for centuries. Hippocrates, the father of modern medicine, proposed the existence of four humors—vital bodily fluids—that govern the health and function of the body. An imbalance of humors (blood, phlegm, yellow bile, and black bile) was believed to cause disease. Centuries later, Galen, another influential Greek physician and philosopher, further developed Hippocrates's theory, proposing four distinct temperaments that each correlated with one of the four humors:

- Sanguine personalities, ruled by blood, were known to be active, enthusiastic, and extroverted.

- Choleric types, ruled by yellow bile, were known to be passionate and irritable.
- Melancholic personalities, ruled by black bile, were typically seen as withdrawn and analytical.
- Phlegmatic types, ruled by phlegm, were seen as relaxed and peaceful.

Surprisingly, some personality systems in existence today continue to utilize these four types as a foundation for understanding personality differences.

During the nineteenth century, physicians began to diagnose mental illness using new language to describe what would later be known as personality disorders. Terms such as moral insanity and mania without delusions were used to describe patients suffering from persistent patterns of internal distress and behavioral dysfunction now associated with personality disorders.

The twentieth century ushered in a greater number of more sophisticated theories on both personality traits and personality disorders. Over time, these various schools of thought resulted in a list of distinct personality disorders that would be organized and printed in the *DSM* (*Diagnostic and Statistical Manual of Mental Disorders*). As of 2021, the *DSM*, now in its fifth edition, identifies ten distinct personality disorders grouped into three clusters (paranoid, schizoid, and schizotypal—cluster A; antisocial, borderline, histrionic, and narcissistic—cluster B; and avoidant, dependent, and obsessive-compulsive—cluster C). Alternative diagnostic systems such as the *Psychodynamic Diagnostic Manual* and Theodore Millon's model recognize other distinct personality disorders not included in the *DSM*, including depressive, self-defeating, and passive-aggressive personality disorders.

Leading experts on personality disorders often disagree about how many categories there are and other issues related to both diagnosis and treatment strategy. The *DSM-V*'s classification system is problematic, due to its near total reliance upon symptoms for diagnosis, not the underlying causes that give rise to chronic problems of personality expression.

CAUSES AND FEATURES

The majority of research on the causes of personality disorders has focused upon childhood abuse and neglect, including inconsistent, invalidating, and chaotic parenting. These factors appear to be the primary risk factors that increase the odds of developing a personality disorder. Genetic contributions have been studied to a lesser extent; initial findings indicate that they also likely play a role in the development of personality disorders.

Typically emerging in late childhood or adolescence (often diagnosed as conduct disorder or oppositional defiant disorder in youth), personality disorders involve rigid patterns of thinking and perception, combined with dysfunctional behaviors and a distorted sense of Self. These patterns differ from what would be considered normal within society, and typically result in a combination of emotional distress and significant functional impairment.

Many people with personality disorders never seek mental health treatment. One explanation for this phenomenon is that personality disorders are what we call ego-syntonic, meaning that the rules that govern the disordered personality are in agreement with the aims of the individual's ego. There are, however, many people with personality disorders who do seek counseling. In some cases, they are looking to address personality issues directly. In many other cases, secondary problems such as depression, anxiety, addictions, and interpersonal problems become the catalyst for seeking help.

ASSESSMENT AND TREATMENT

If you have reason to believe that you may be suffering from a personality disorder, ask your therapist to assess you for this issue. It's important to note that, as with many other mental health problems, personality disorders fall on a spectrum. This range includes having only traits of a personality disorder, as well as mild, moderate, and severe cases. One of my favorite colleagues claims that everyone has a personality disorder. In other words, we all have parts of our personality that are inflexible, that often cause us emotional suffering and interpersonal problems.

Treatment for personality disorders is typically long term, gradual, and in depth. With curiosity and determination, however, it is possible to make subtle—but meaningful—changes to your personality structure. These changes can help to resolve some of the underlying depression, anxiety, and social problems that frequently come along with personality disorders. In addition to individual therapy, other treatment modalities available include dialectical behavior therapy (DBT), which involves a combination of cognitive behavioral therapy, mindfulness practices, and skills building through group therapy. DBT was originally developed to address borderline personality disorder (BPD), which for years was seen as responding poorly to treatment.

Personality disorders can often be overlooked, though they often play a large role in other mental health problems. Having an accurate diagnosis and a clear treatment plan while working with a therapist who has a deep understanding of personality dynamics can make a positive impact upon therapy outcomes. Each personality disorder requires a different treatment approach. A holistic treatment plan is ideal, as meditation and other experiential activities are often necessary to supplement traditional psychotherapy.

Chapter Thirty-Nine

Procrastination

Let's face it. Everyone procrastinates from time to time. It's human nature to put off until later tasks that are either boring or stressful. As a matter of fact, I put off writing this chapter of the book until just before it went into production. In many cases, the act of procrastination turns out to be nothing more than a minor irritation, a brief bout of elevated stress that resolves once the deadline has been met. On the other hand, there are instances of procrastination that result in serious consequences and profound emotional suffering. If issues of procrastination and motivation have plagued your life, read on.

TWO KINDS OF PROCRASTINATION

Your first step is to determine what kind of procrastinator you are. Throughout my career, I have worked with two types of procrastinators—eleventh-hour procrastinators and self-defeating procrastinators. The first group are made up of people who get things done at the last minute. While often caught up in a frenzied state of distress, they nearly always find a way to make it to the finish line. The second group's procrastination tendencies lead to missed deadlines and lost opportunities. As you can imagine, while both groups may begin projects and endeavors with similar patterns of delay and distraction, their outcomes are quite different.

Therapy for the eleventh-hour procrastinator will require a much different course than therapy for the self-defeating procrastinator. Having worked with your therapist to determine which kind of procrastinator you are, you can move forward with the best treatment approach for your particular situation and corresponding goals.

ELEVENTH-HOUR PROCRASTINATION

You get things done—at the last minute. Unlike your colleagues and classmates who plan ahead and have their work completed a week in advance, you are more apt to pull an all-nighter to complete a term paper, to write your Sunday sermon late Saturday evening, to put the finishing touches on your PowerPoint presentation minutes before walking into the big meeting that has been on your calendar for weeks. Meeting deadlines in this way is often a combination of thrilling and exhausting. You may have even promised yourself that, next time, you will start sooner, that you will never put yourself in such a crunch again.

If this describes you, you may be surprised to learn that therapy will most likely focus on accepting your work style. The quality of your work is on par with your ahead-of-schedule counterparts. Why not accept that procrastination is a part of your process? Trying to change yourself in fundamental ways may cause you more harm than good.

If, however, the effects of your procrastination are detrimental—causing you excessive anxiety, tension, and insomnia—you can work with your therapist on fine-tuning your procrastination style. Your goals could include moderating certain aspects of your eleventh-hour practices, while still honoring and accepting your basic nature.

To summarize, therapy for this form of procrastination involves

- Understanding your productivity style,
- Accepting that you will continue to procrastinate,
- Letting go of any guilty feelings about this issue, and
- Modifying habits that cause significant problems or distress.

SELF-DEFEATING PROCRASTINATION

If you frequently miss deadlines, fail to complete projects, and miss out on opportunities that are important to you, then your style of procrastination has become self-defeating. Therapy for your situation will involve a different set of questions and objectives. For example, you and your therapist can explore the following avenues to identify the source of the problem:

- Undiagnosed conditions, including addictions, ADHD, anxiety, dyslexia, bipolar disorder, and others
- Fear of failure
- Fear of success
- Passive-aggressive behavior
- Perfectionism
- Unresolved trauma

Each of these issues can contribute to you sabotaging your own efforts. And each of these issues is unique, thus requiring a specialized treatment plan. The truth is, if you are consistently getting in your own way, there is a missing puzzle piece that needs to be discovered and addressed in order to help you to succeed. Together, you and your therapist can explore the root causes of your self-defeating procrastination. Once the source of the problem has been correctly identified, you can move forward with your treatment plan.

ASK YOUR THERAPIST

When attempting to make behavioral changes, I always recommend that you start by tracking what you are currently doing. Don't change anything yet. Take two weeks to make detailed observations of your target behavior. Record your findings in a journal, notebook, or digital device. Your task is to **notice as much as you can, without any judgment**. Keep your goals in mind as you make notes on your observations. Be on the lookout for patterns. After you establish your baseline, you can implement a strategy to help you change your behaviors and reach your goals.

Given that there is no one-size-fits-all approach to overcoming procrastination, it is important to choose a system and stick with it. One sure way to hold yourself back is to repeatedly fall in love with the latest self-help fad, while abandoning practices that, though not perfect, are working for you. To think of it another way, you will never reach the top of the mountain if you spend your time exploring only the first mile of the many available trails. Better to pick one trail and follow it to the end.

CHAPTER FORTY

Relationship Problems

THIS CHAPTER COVERS relationship problems that can be addressed individually, as well as counseling for couples and families. When your relationships are in trouble and cease to function, it is time to get professional help. Therapy for relationship issues can either be short or long term, depending on the nature and the severity of the problem.

INDIVIDUAL THERAPY

Perhaps you want to break free from a self-defeating relationship pattern. Or maybe your goal is to become more assertive in your current relationships. Are you afraid of intimacy and commitment, constantly running away from people who love you? Do you have painful memories of past lovers who have left you with wounds that never properly healed?

All of these issues respond well to individual therapy. Therapy will allow you to explore these questions in depth, to gain an understanding of yourself in relation to others, and to develop a new relationship skill set. With a greater awareness of your own relationship style and improved relationship skills, you can look forward to greater satisfaction in your relationships with others.

While individual therapy for relationship issues can go in a lot of different directions, a few roads are worth exploring for nearly every client. These include

- Examination of your family of origin,
- Examination of your past relationships, and
- Examination of your defense mechanisms.

Examining these facets of your past will allow you to become more conscious of how you function in your present relationships and, with hard work, can pave the way for new roads to be traveled.

COUPLES COUNSELING

Working with a marriage or couples counselor differs from individual therapy in many important ways. For starters, your therapist has three clients to consider: you, your partner, and your relationship. Sessions for couples typically have a very different format and feel to them than individual sessions.

While your couples counselor will be providing empathy at times, there are many more occasions where you will be confronted with critical feedback. Your therapist will seek to understand your point of view as well as that of your partner. Keeping both sets of feelings, experiences, and needs in mind, your therapist will attempt to guide you both toward a middle ground. They will facilitate healthy communication, teach expression of empathy, assist with hard conversations, and reframe conflicts in new ways.

Counseling for couples works best when it begins early. Some couples pursue premarital counseling to identify potential problems and learn relationship skills early on. Other couples come into therapy when their problems are small, seeking professional guidance to help them talk through difficult issues and teach better communication skills. And yet many more couples seek marriage counseling once they are in crisis, overwhelmed with hurt feelings, anger, disconnection, and resentment—resentments that, in many cases, have festered for years.

Regardless of where your relationship is currently, if you and your partner both have a sincere desire to address your issues, combined with a commitment to the hard work required, it's not too late to get help. Approaching couples counseling with an open mind and a courageous heart will help you tremendously in reaping the greatest possible rewards from the process. For more detailed information, see part III on relationships.

FAMILY THERAPY

Resolution of family conflict often requires the introduction of a novel character into the family system. When you enter family therapy, your therapist becomes a temporary member of your family system, thus creating a new dynamic.

While it's often the case that one family member is the focus of family therapy—often a child with behavioral and attitude problems—change can only occur when all members of the family make an investment in the process, taking an honest look at themselves.

In many cases, family issues can be resolved rather quickly by following behavioral suggestions given by the therapist. In other cases, multiple family members may need to engage in individual therapy while also participating in family therapy. Regardless of your family situation, it is important to approach family therapy with an open mind and a willingness to address each member's contribution to the family dynamic.

The quality of our relationships to others plays a large role in our sense of well-being and can even impact the quality of our health. Taking the time to learn and grow in relationships is one of the most worthwhile endeavors a person can pursue. While it does require emotional risks as well as the significant investment of time, the potential for great rewards is tremendous.

Chapter Forty-One

Self-Destructive Behavior

Self-destructive behavior can take many forms. For some, it manifests as compulsive cutting and other physical attacks on the body. Others harm themselves through chronically sabotaging their relationships or their careers. And, of course, there is the slow burn of bad habits—smoking, excessive drinking, poor diet, neglecting self-care, avoiding medical check-ups, and the list goes on.

Self-destructive behavior can also take the form of risky behavior, especially for those who feel driven by the impulse to flirt with danger at every turn. No matter how it manifests, self-harming behaviors are clearly problematic and at odds with the goals of personal growth and well-being.

WHY WE DO THE THINGS WE DO

Why do we do things that are bad for us? There is no universal way to answer this question. The truth is, people engage in self-destructive behaviors for a variety of reasons, such as these most common reasons:

- To feel numb
- To act out emotional pain

- Due to addiction
- To attempt to repair past trauma through repetition
- To push others away
- As a result of undiagnosed neurological conditions

It is quite common for a combination of these factors to coexist and feed off each other. What can be done about this? Therapy for self-destructive behavior is often part of a larger course of treatment designed to resolve the effects of trauma. Most self-destructive behavior is a symptom of deeper injury, an emotional wound in need of healing. As such, it is important to cast a wide net when attempting to understand and overcome self-destructive patterns. If therapy is focused only on symptom reduction, you risk manifesting new forms of self-harm if the underlying issue has not been sufficiently addressed.

THE TASKS OF THERAPY

Some examples of the tasks of therapy for self-destructive behavior include

- Identifying and expressing repressed emotions,
- Learning to tolerate the experience of emotional vulnerability,
- Transforming distorted narratives about the Self into empowering ones,
- Replacing self-destructive habits with healthy outlets for self-care, and
- Increasing self-awareness through mindfulness practice.

Over time, with patience, curiosity, and hard work, you can learn to transform self-destructive patterns into life-affirming ones.

Chapter Forty-Two

Self-Esteem Problems

The notion that self-esteem is critical to one's well-being and success is uniquely American. According to some sources, our national self-esteem craze was born from the pet project of an eccentric California politician in the 1980s. The movement took off, cementing the importance of self-esteem in the American psyche.

A FLAWED CONCEPT

The millennial generation are the guinea pigs of this grand social experiment that sought to constantly fortify the self-esteem of children, both at home and at school. The self-esteem craze created a culture where everyone is special and everybody gets a trophy. Much of what was originally believed about self-esteem was later found to be oversimplified at best and, in some cases, wrong. For example, many psychopaths generally have high levels of self-esteem, discrediting the notion that increased self-esteem will discourage crime.

While a complete deconstruction of the self-esteem movement is beyond the scope of this chapter, it is important to establish the foundation that self-esteem is, in many ways, a problematic concept.

SELF-ESTEEM VERSUS SELF-CONFIDENCE

Self-esteem is defined as one's subjective appraisal of their own worth; in other words, it is a measurement of your level of self-respect. This differs from self-confidence, which has to do with your feeling of competence in specific areas (arts, athletics, academics, and other achievements).

There are many individuals with high confidence in their abilities who have low self-esteem. In fact, this phenomenon is quite common, as many people with low self-esteem seek more and greater achievements in the hope of ameliorating painful insecurities. And while the concept of self-esteem is problematic, it is deeply rooted in our shared heritage and language, and so we must reckon with it.

Poor self-esteem, like many other mental health concerns, is very often the result of unresolved developmental trauma. Consequently, treatment of self-esteem problems requires an accurate assessment followed by the long, hard work of sorting through the memories and emotions that created a distorted view of the Self in the first place (see chapter 43 on trauma and PTSD for more information). There are, however, some themes and concepts I have found helpful in overcoming self-esteem problems.

HONEST INVENTORY OF STRENGTHS AND WEAKNESSES

People with poor self-esteem frequently both undervalue and overvalue personal traits and abilities. You cannot have a healthy relationship with yourself if you are engaged in self-deception. Once you begin to accept your limitations and take ownership of your talents, you can begin to relate to yourself honestly and with compassion.

MEANINGFUL PURSUITS, AUTHENTICITY, AND SELF-COMPASSION

Spending time on meaningful pursuits has a way of raising your positive sense of Self. The real benefit to self-esteem comes when your pursuits are done in the service of your own desires, not based on obligation to others or on a never-ending quest for praise. Furthermore, when you express yourself authentically, positive feelings tend to follow. Some self-esteem problems can be resolved by identifying and removing blockages to authentic self-expression. Ultimately, a fundamental shift in attitude toward the Self is necessary. For many, the development of self-compassion can be quite difficult. While it may be a lifelong endeavor, it is a foundational practice. As the wise psychologist Carl Rogers once said, "The curious paradox is that when I accept myself just as I am, then I can change."

HEALTHY RELATIONSHIPS

The quality of your relationships has a tremendous impact on your mental health. If you are suffering from poor self-esteem, take stock of the people in your life. Do they treat you well? Do they treat you with respect? If the answer is no, then change is in order.

These concepts are starting points for your journey of transforming low self-esteem into compassion and kindness toward yourself.

Chapter Forty-Three

Trauma and PTSD

Many of the psychological issues people face can be traced back to traumatic experiences of one kind or another. Understanding the full scope of trauma's impact as well as the dynamics of recovery is fundamental to the healing journey.

Since the 1970s, there has been a steady stream of research on trauma, accompanied by the development of novel treatment methods for posttraumatic stress disorder (PTSD). Originally called *shell shock* during World War I, our understanding of PTSD has evolved over time. Today, clinicians and researchers have a deeper understanding of trauma dynamics and access to a wider array of therapies.

TRAUMA DEFINED

Trauma is an emotional and physiological reaction to a terrible or overwhelming experience. Psychological trauma can result from a single event or from a chronic source of stress. The extent of trauma's impact upon your life depends on a host of factors, including

- The age at which trauma occurred,
- The intensity of the experience,

- The frequency of the experience,
- Whether or not you received support following trauma, and
- Personality variables.

Not everyone who experiences trauma develops PTSD. As a matter of fact, most do not. In many cases, however, traumatic experiences are cumulative, like a snowball that grows bigger as it rolls down the mountainside. When traumatic experiences accumulate in this way, and remain untreated, the effects can become more serious. To make sense of the many ways traumatic experiences can linger on, we must first organize our approach.

BIG "T" AND LITTLE "T" TRAUMA

Many clinicians divide trauma into big T and little t trauma. Examples of big T trauma include being the victim of rape or violence; being abused (verbal, mental, physical, sexual, or financial); living through war or natural disasters; experiencing profound physical and emotional neglect; witnessing violence to others; surviving a serious motor vehicle accident; living through medical trauma; and any other overwhelming experience.

Examples of little t trauma include divorce; repeated relocation; being bullied; being invalidated by parents or other caregivers; being the victim of cruel teachers or coaches; experiencing systemic racism, sexism, homophobia, transphobia, and other forms of discrimination; and any other harsh treatment. Little t trauma can also include repeated exposure to chaotic and stressful situations while young and impressionable.

Both big T and little t trauma can cause a person to develop significant psychological problems. For some, the impact of trauma is short-lived, while for others, the damage persists for years.

Symptoms that accompany trauma range from numbness to panic, from hypervigilance to dissociation. Anxiety, depression, nightmares, flashbacks, social avoidance, shame, and substance abuse are some of the most common symptoms of posttraumatic stress.

In addition to these symptoms, trauma can change the way you think about the world, as well as how you conduct yourself in relationships. For example, your view of the future may become bleak and pessimistic. It's not uncommon to develop distorted perceptions, misinterpreting the neutral actions of others as malicious or threatening. Trusting others can be difficult, and relationship difficulties are more common when unresolved trauma is present.

Given the fact that trauma affects people on multiple dimensions—physical, psychological, and spiritual—any effective trauma treatment must be holistic. Here is a breakdown of the effects of trauma and the mechanisms of healing.

PHYSICAL

Trauma directly impacts the nervous system. Depending on what developmental stage you're in at the time of traumatic experience, the degree of impact on the developing nervous system will be different.

Multiple studies have shown a strong correlation between traumatic experiences in childhood (as measured by the Adverse Childhood Experience scale) and increased risk of developing a host of physical health problems in later life. In his book, *The Body Keeps the Score*, Bessel van der Kolk details the ways that developmental trauma changes how a person experiences basic bodily functions, including sleeping, eating, and elimination.

Given these discoveries, healing the after-effects of trauma requires working directly with your body. It has been said that *our issues are in the tissues.* Methods for healing trauma on a physical level include breathing exercises, yoga, martial arts, and other forms of physical exercise. The goal is twofold: (1) you must learn to establish safety in your immediate environment, and (2) you must learn to regulate your nervous system through breath control, mindfulness, and movement.

In many cases, the development of physical abilities (strength and athleticism) and the mastery of self-defense (martial arts and possibly weapons training) can play an important role in healing. If you were physically abused or controlled by others, it can be very empowering to develop the ability to protect yourself physically.

Receiving healing touch from another is also an important part of the healing process; massage and other forms of bodywork are excellent choices for this.

Specialized therapies, including eye movement desensitization and reprocessing (EMDR), neurofeedback, and the Somatic Experiencing method can also be quite helpful for addressing the neurological effects of posttraumatic stress. Many trauma therapists have received training and certification in these specialized modalities.

MENTAL AND EMOTIONAL

Human beings are storytellers. As we grow up, mature, and eventually grow old, we tell ourselves many stories. These include stories about the world, stories about ourselves, and stories about what is possible. Our stories change over time, as we are shaped by the important people in our lives, as well as by the memorable experiences we have along the way.

Experiences such as abandonment, harsh treatment, abuse, recurrent losses, and disaster can alter and corrupt our stories. These same experiences can also obstruct our ability to feel and express our emotions, creating energetic blockages and imbalances. This combination of mental and emotional consequences is another way cumulative traumatic experiences play out, often leading to the development of psychological symptoms. *A constricted world view, combined with chronic emotional repression, is the single biggest underlying cause of the anxiety, depression, anger, and other issues that typically lead a person into therapy.*

Positively rewriting your internal narrative and learning to correctly identify and express your emotions is the bread and butter of psychotherapy. Make no mistake—this journey can be long and difficult. The rewards, however, are tremendous. An effective therapist with whom you have a good working relationship can help you to explore, understand, and ultimately transform your thoughts, beliefs, and attitudes. They can also support you in developing a healthy relationship with your emotional life. This alone can bring tremendous healing to the trauma of the past.

BEHAVIORAL

In an effort to protect ourselves, both physically and emotionally, we often acquire self-destructive behaviors. A central part of the treatment of trauma involves replacing these old coping patterns with new, more functional forms of self-care. In order to successfully do this, your therapy must first get to the bottom of the underlying causes of the behavior.

One of the many therapy models that are effective for trauma is called Internal Family Systems (IFS), which posits that inside each of us we have many parts. Some parts are young and wounded, while others are older, acting as protectors. While there is a lot of complexity to this dynamic, the bottom line is that many self-destructive behaviors are the work of certain protective parts that are trying to shield your inner child from overwhelming emotional pain. While these behavioral dynamics may have served you in the past, chances are, they are now hindering your growth.

Whether your self-protective instincts manifest in socially accepted forms such as perfectionism and workaholism, or self-destructive forms such as addictions and acting out, it is likely they have outlasted their usefulness. Gaining insight into these behavioral patterns is a crucial step toward healing.

In order for lasting change to occur, however, insights must be backed up by a commitment to action. You and your therapist can explore exactly how to transform these behaviors into new, healthy ones. Relapse is a part of recovery, so do not expect this journey to look like a straight line. But with courage, curiosity, and commitment, new behaviors can be established and sustained.

RELATIONAL

Given that trauma frequently occurs within the context of relationships, so too does the healing occur within relationships. This is why the selection of your therapist is very important. Choosing someone whom you trust, someone with whom you can develop a working alliance, is key to working though trauma.

In the best of cases, a corrective emotional experience can occur through the therapeutic relationship. You can also experience healing in your relationships with friends, lovers, mentors, and other key people in your life. Cultivating healing relationships requires the ability to determine who is worthy of your trust, the capacity to be vulnerable, and the willingness to tolerate the limitations of others. This process is often one of trial and error. Understanding that relationships are key to healing trauma is of the utmost importance.

SPIRITUAL

Many wise teachers have suggested that awe is what characterizes the spiritual experience. Regardless of your world view or religious beliefs, awe is a universal part of the human experience. Awe can be directed toward things both great and small:

- The mystery of life
- The wonders of nature
- The beauty of colors and sounds
- The way late afternoon sun casts golden light upon the trees
- The laughter of children
- A sublime piece of music
- A surprising coincidence
- Simple pleasures

Sadly, trauma can diminish your ability to experience awe. This happens when you become singularly focused on survival. The path of healing has frequently been described as going from a state of surviving to a state of thriving. Or as Maya Angelou once said, "My mission in life is not merely to survive, but to thrive; and to do so with some passion, compassion, some humor, and some style."

Many studies show that people with a strong tie to a religious faith tradition are more resilient in the face of trauma and adversity. In my experience, clients who are able to find a source of deeper meaning in their lives are better able to contextualize and integrate the legacy of past trauma. Some practical applications of this principle include these:

- Being part of a community
- Prayer
- Meditation
- Yoga
- Developing a life-affirming world view
- Finding solace in nature
- A commitment to service
- Living with purpose

Another example of a spiritual solution to healing trauma includes the use of expressive arts, like writing, visual art, or music. If you want, they can be used in conjunction with personalized rituals designed to symbolize your journey of transformation. This process requires you to follow your instincts and is very personal and individualistic.

Embarking upon the journey of healing trauma may appear daunting and overwhelming. Take comfort in the knowledge that you will not have to make this journey alone; if you ask for help, there will be allies to join you along your way. You may be pleasantly surprised to find that your greatest challenges give rise to new gifts and greater compassion. Indeed, many of the world's greatest voices and most devoted spiritual seekers are those who have found a way to transform their pain into purpose. As Lao Tzu said, "A journey of a thousand miles begins with a single step."

A Hopeful Future

OUR JOURNEY TOGETHER is coming to an end. We have covered lots of ground through the pages of the book, and perhaps you have explored new terrain in your own therapy. Although each reader will resonate with different ideas, there are several core concepts that I hope you take away from our time together:

- There is no one-size-fits-all solution to psychological problems and relationship issues.
- Finding a skillful guide, a therapist you connect with, will make your journey both more comfortable and more fulfilling.
- The more that you put into the process—including courage, dedication, honesty, curiosity, and a willingness to go the extra mile—the more you will get out of it.
- There are many powerful tools, resources, and practices available to complement your healing journey, including nature, physical exercise, yoga, meditation, art, music, writing, martial arts, massage therapy, chiropractic care, nutrition, and others.
- The quality of your relationships with your loved ones plays a significant role in your psychological well-being.

- Learning to slow down and get to know yourself at a deeper level is one of the most effective ways you can strengthen your relationships with others.
- Your psychotherapy journey may involve more than one episode of care with more than one therapist. You may find that you are able to get different insights, points of view, and resources from different therapists.

I sincerely hope that you have found the elements you were looking for on your journey thus far. The world of psychotherapy and mental health care is vast, with much to offer. If there are roads and trails left unexplored, I encourage you to continue your quest, wherever it may lead you. Many of the chapters in this book could be complete books unto themselves. If something new piqued your interest, I hope that you will explore further. You may also want to take a look at the Further Reading section to see some of my personal favorites on a variety of topics.

Many blessings on your journey.

End Notes

INTRODUCTION

Symes, William. *Mastering the Art of Psychotherapy*. Green Writers Press, 2016.

CHAPTER 2

Miller, Scott, Mark Hubble, and Barry Duncan. *The Secrets of Supershrinks: Pathways to Clinical Excellence.* Psychotherapy Networker, 2008.

Wampold, B. E. and G. S. Brown. "Estimating variability in outcomes attributable to therapists: A naturalistic study of outcomes in managed care." *Journal of Consulting and Clinical Psychology*, Volume 73, 5:914–23.

CHAPTER 4

Blanchard, Matt and Barry A. Farber. "Lying in psychotherapy: Why and what clients don't tell their therapist about therapy and their relationship." *Counselling Psychology Quarterly,* Volume 29, 2015 - 1-23. 10.1080/09515070.2015.1085365.

CHAPTER 8

Pollan, Michael. *How to Change Your Mind*. New York: Penguin Press, 2018.

Walker, Matthew. *Why We Sleep*. New York: Scribner, 2017.

CHAPTER 9

Cameron, Julia. *The Artist's Way*. New York: Jeremy P. Tarcher/Perigee, 1992.

Fromm, Erich, D. T. Suzuki, and Richard De Martino. *Zen Buddhism and Psychoanalysis*. New York: Harper and Brothers, 1960.

Haley, Jay. *Uncommon Therapy*. New York: W. W. Norton & Company, 1993.

Rubin, Gretchen. *Better Than Before*. New York: Crown, 2015.

Suzuki, Shunryu. *Zen Mind, Beginner's Mind*. New York: Weatherhill, 2007.

van der Kolk, Bessel. *The Body Keeps the Score*. New York: Viking, 2014.

CHAPTER 10

Jung, C. G. *On the Nature of the Psyche*. New York: Bollingen Foundation, 1960.

Singer, June. *Boundaries of the Soul*. New York: Anchor Books, 1994.

CHAPTER 11

Arbinger Institute. *Leadership and Self-Deception*. San Francisco, CA: Berrett-Koehler Publishers, 2002.

CHAPTER 12

Csikszentmihalyi, Mihaly. *Flow*. New York: HarperPerennial, 1991.

Gilbert, Daniel. *Stumbling on Happiness*. New York: Vintage Books, 2007.

Manson, Mark. *The Subtle Art of Not Giving a F*ck*. New York: HarperOne, 2016.

CHAPTER 13

Brown, Brené. *Dare to Lead*. New York: Random House, 2018.

Frankl, Viktor, *Man's Search for Meaning*. Boston: Beacon Press, 2006.

Trungpa, Chögyam. *Cutting Through Spiritual Materialism*. Boulder, CO: Shambhala Publications, 1973.

CHAPTER 14

Campbell, Joseph. *The Hero with a Thousand Faces*. Princeton, NJ: Princeton University Press, 1973.

CHAPTER 16

Ulrich, Roger. "View through a window may influence recovery from surgery." *Science* 1984, May; 224(4647):420–1.

Williams, Florence. *The Nature Fix*. New York: W.W. Norton, 2017.

CHAPTER 17

Symes, William. *Mastering the Art of Psychotherapy*. Green Writers Press, 2016.

Van de Castle, Robert. *Our Dreaming Mind*. New York: Ballantine Books, 1995.

Walker, Matthew. *Why We Sleep*. New York: Scribner, 2017.

CHAPTER 20

Perel, Esther. *Mating in Captivity*. New York: Harper Collins, 2006.

Real, Terrence. *The New Rules of Marriage*. New York: Ballantine Books, 2008.

Tatkin, Stan. *Wired for Love*. Oakland, CA: New Harbinger, 2012.

CHAPTER 21

Simsion, Graeme. *The Rosie Project.* New York: Simon & Schuster, 2013.

CHAPTER 22

Stone, Douglas, Bruce Patton, and Sheila Heen of the Harvard Negotiation Project. *Difficult Conversations.* New York: Penguin Books, 2010.

CHAPTER 25

Archer, Dale. *The ADHD Advantage*. New York: Avery, 2016.

Hallowell, Edward M. and John J. Ratey. *Driven to Distraction.* New York: Anchor Books, 2011.

Louv, Richard. *Last Child in the Woods*. Chapel Hill, NC: Algonquin Books, 2008.

CHAPTER 28

Silberman, Steve. *NeuroTribes.* New York: Avery, 2016.

CHAPTER 31

Real, Terrence. *I Don't Want to Talk About It.* New York: Scribner, 1998.

CHAPTER 34

Bach, Richard. *Illusions.* Tulsa, OK: Gardners Books, 2001.

Brown, Brené. *Daring Greatly.* New York: Avery, 2012.

CHAPTER 36

Hance, Jeremy. *Baggage: Tales of a Globe-Trotting Hypochondriac.* Deerfield Beach, FL: Health Communications, Inc., 2020.

CHAPTER 37

Fay, Jim and Charles Fay. *Love and Logic Magic for Early Childhood.* Golden, CO: Love and Logic Institute, Inc., 2000.

CHAPTER 43

van der Kolk, Bessel. *The Body Keeps the Score.* New York: Viking, 2014.

Further Reading

PSYCHOLOGICAL WELL-BEING

Brown, Brené. *Daring Greatly*. New York: Avery, 2012.

Gilbert, Daniel. *Stumbling on Happiness*. New York: Vintage Books, 2007.

Holiday, Ryan and Stephen Hanselman. *The Daily Stoic*. New York: Portfolio, 2016.

Manson, Mark. *The Subtle Art of Not Giving a F*ck*. New York: HarperOne, 2016.

Pearson, Carol. *The Hero Within*. New York: HarperCollins, 1998.

Walker, Matthew. *Why We Sleep*. New York: Scribner, 2017.

Watts, Alan. *The Wisdom of Insecurity*. New York: Pantheon, 1958.

Williams, Florence. *The Nature Fix*. New York: W.W. Norton, 2017.

RELATIONSHIPS

Gottman, John and Nan Silver. *The Seven Principles for Making Marriage Work*. New York: Harmony Books, 2015.

Kirshenbaum, Mira. *Too Good to Leave, Too Bad to Stay*. New York: Plume, 1997.

Perel, Esther. *Mating in Captivity*. New York: HarperCollins, 2006.

Real, Terrence. *The New Rules of Marriage*. New York: Ballantine Books, 2008.

Tatkin, Stan. *Wired for Love*. Oakland, CA: New Harbinger, 2012.

ON BEING IN THERAPY

Gottlieb, Lori. *Maybe You Should Talk to Someone*. New York: Houghton Mifflin Harcourt, 2019.

Yalom, Irvin. *Creatures of a Day*. New York: Basic Books, 2015.

MINDFULNESS AND MEDITATION

Kabat-Zinn, Jon. *Wherever You Go, There You Are*. New York: MJF Books, 2005.

ADHD

Archer, Dale. *The ADHD Advantage*. New York: Avery, 2016.

Hallowell, Edward M. and John J. Ratey. *Driven to Distraction*. New York: Anchor Books, 2011.

ADDICTIONS

Grisel, Judith. *Never Enough*. New York: Doubleday, 2019.

Johnson, Vernon. *I'll Quit Tomorrow*. New York: Harper Collins, 1990.

Maté, Gabor. *In the Realm of Hungry Ghosts*. Berkeley, CA: North Atlantic Books, 2010.

ANGER

Potter-Efron, Ronald and Patricia Potter-Efron. *Letting Go of Anger.* Oakland, CA: New Harbinger Publications, 2007.

AUTISM AND ASPERGER SYNDROME

Attwood, Tony. *The Complete Guide to Asperger's Syndrome.* London: Jessica Kingsley Publishers, 2008.

Grandin, Temple. *The Way I See It.* Arlington, TX: Future Horizons, 2020.

Silberman, Steve. *NeuroTribes.* New York: Avery, 2016.

CODEPENDENCY

Mellody, Pia. *Facing Codependence.* New York: HarperOne, 2003.

DEPRESSION

Burns, David. *Feeling Good.* William Morrow & Co, 1980.

Real, Terrence. *I Don't Want to Talk About It.* New York: Scribner, 1998.

Seligman, Martin. *Learned Optimism.* New York: Vintage Books, 2006.

DIFFICULT PEOPLE

Lester, Gregory. *Power with People.* Ashcroft Press, 2014.

Stout, Martha. *The Sociopath Next Door.* New York: Broadway Books, 2005.

PARENTING

Martin, William. *The Parent's Tao Te Ching*. Cambridge, MA: Da Capo Press, 1999.

PROCRASTINATION AND PRODUCTIVITY

Allen, David. *Getting Things Done*. New York: Penguin Books, 2015.

Rubin, Gretchen. *Better Than Before*. New York: Crown, 2015.

SHAME

Brown, Brené. *Daring Greatly*. New York: Avery, 2012.

TRAUMA

Frankl, Viktor, *Man's Search for Meaning*. Boston: Beacon Press, 2006.

Levine, Peter, with Ann Frederick. *Waking the Tiger*. Berkeley, CA: North Atlantic Books, 1997.

van der Kolk, Bessel. *The Body Keeps the Score*. New York: Viking, 2014.

Acknowledgments

Much like being in therapy, writing a book—especially for the first time—is a journey of discovery. I am deeply grateful for the path I have found myself on, and for the gracious support of friends, family, colleagues, and collaborators who helped me along the way.

First, I would like to express my deepest appreciation to my wife, Sarah. I am ever grateful for your endless support and encouragement and for listening to my caffeinated early morning ramblings. You believed in me and my idea from day one, patiently reading through draft after draft, offering many insightful comments and suggestions. You are simply the best!

Next, I would like to thank my editor, Gabrielle Moss. Many thanks for your editorial comments, insightful suggestions, and your confidence in my book.

Mad props to my friend Greg Moore for creating a beautiful cover design. You really hit the nail on the head.

Early in my writing process, as my ideas were just beginning to form, I reached out to my uncle Mike Newman, my uncle Jim Smith, and my longtime family friend Tom Tomshany for both feedback and editorial help. Each of you gave me key input, including insightful editorial comments and much-needed encouragement. Those early conversations kept me on track. My deepest appreciation to each of you for your generosity of time, for your good ideas, and your wise counsel.

A hearty thank-you goes out to my friend Jeremy Hance for helping me to navigate the new and unfamiliar maze of agents, publishers, and the whole damn business of being a writer. Your guidance was invaluable.

To my dear friends and colleagues in Fayetteville—Jon Medders, Kathleen Wong, and Stacey Bailey—thank you for reading over my book with your clinical hats on. I am ever grateful for your friendship and our ongoing conversations about this strange and wonderful profession.

A Razorback-sized thank-you to my dear friend and mentor Bill Symes for his many contributions to my professional development. Beginning with our first meeting in April 2004, you have again and again showed me the true power of therapy. I owe you a tremendous amount of gratitude for all that you have shared of yourself. I would not be the therapist that I am today without your wise and generous support. Thank you also for reviewing my manuscript and providing helpful feedback.

To my parents, Patrick and Jane Newman, I am eternally grateful. You have always supported and encouraged me to be my true Self and to have the courage and conviction to pursue my dreams. Thank you also for modeling how to live a meaningful life, grounded in my core values. I am so thankful for all that you have given me.

To my sister, Emily Christie, and my brother-in-law, Thomas Christie, my deepest appreciation for your love, support, and friendship.

To my grad school crew—Jamie McDonnell, Mark Lersch, Karen Kral, Greg McNeil, Niccole Toral, Tod DiCecco, Jeff Stahl, Christina Forde, Ralph Lind, Deb Heikes, and the rest of the gang at Southwestern College—it was a blast figuring out how to be therapists together. And to my first mentor and clinical supervisor, Larry Dettweiler, a deep bow of gratitude for your guidance and support in my early days as a fledgling therapist.

My undergraduate psychology professors at Hendrix College watered the seeds of my intellectual curiosity and fostered my love of psychology. A heartfelt thank-you to Ralph McKenna, Tim Maxwell, and Chris Spatz for your infectious enthusiasm and your engaging teaching style. My love and commitment to applied psychology goes straight back to my days in the Mills Building.

A very special note of appreciation to my son, Nathan. Your bright spirit and tenacious conviction are an inspiration to me. Being your father has been one of the greatest experiences of my life. As I find my way along the wild adventure of parenthood, you help me to be a better person, and a better therapist.

To the therapists who have helped me over the years, I am deeply grateful. You showed me the good that therapy can do. Your warmth, insight, professionalism, and care meant the world to me during my time of need.

And finally, a deep debt of gratitude belongs to my clients, both past and present. You have trusted me to be your guide as you navigate the changes in your lives. It's been an honor to make the journey with you, and it's you whom I learn from the most.

About the Author

Joshua Newman is a licensed professional clinical counselor (LPCC) in private practice. With over twenty years of mental health care experience, he has provided psychological counseling to hundreds of individuals, couples, and families. In his practice, Joshua integrates principles of contemporary Western psychology with the ancient wisdom of Eastern philosophy. He holds a bachelor of arts in psychology and religion from Hendrix College and a master of arts in counseling from Southwestern College.

Over the course of his career, he has presented numerous lectures on psychology, psychotherapy, dreams, and meditation. Joshua was first introduced to meditation practice by the late Zen Master Keido Fukushima Roshi during a religion class in college. He has attempted to maintain a meditation practice ever since.

When he is not at work, he can be found playing his bass guitar, watching basketball, or enjoying the great outdoors. He lives in Albuquerque, New Mexico, with his wife and son. To learn more, visit www.janewman.com.